OUTSIDE
THE
JUKEBOX

SCOTT BRADLEE

OUTSIDE
THE
JUKEBOX

HOW I TURNED MY VINTAGE MUSIC
OBSESSION INTO MY DREAM GIG

SCOTT BRADLEE

hachette
BOOKS

NEW YORK   BOSTON

Hachette Books
Hachette Book Group
1290 Avenue of the Americas
New York, NY 10104
hachettebookgroup.com

twitter.com/hachettebooks

First Edition: June 2018

Hachette Books is a division of Hachette Book Group, Inc.

The Hachette Books name and logo are trademarks of Hachette Book Group, Inc.

The publisher is not responsible for websites (or their content) that are not owned by the publisher.

The Hachette Speakers Bureau provides a wide range of authors for speaking events. To find out more, go to www.hachettespeakersbureau.com or call (866) 376-6591.

Insert photos are courtesy of Scott Bradlee, except as follows:
    p. 1, bottom: © Adam Brown
    p. 2, top: © Michelle Hayes
    p. 2, bottom: © Paul Madrinan

Library of Congress Control Number: 2018934274

ISBNs: 978-0-316-41573-6 (hardcover), 978-0-316-41572-9 (ebook)

Printed in the United States of America

LSC-C

10 9 8 7 6 5 4 3 2 1

CONTENTS

CONTENTS

CONTENTS

PREFACE

My name is Scott Bradlee.

I grew up in rural New Jersey, in a small town, in a middle-class family. We lived in an unassuming house and did unassuming things, like watch *Jeopardy!*, play *Scrabble*, and go for after-dinner walks down to the end of the cul-de-sac on which we lived.

We didn't have any relatives in the entertainment industry, and none of us had ever been west of Pennsylvania, let alone to Hollywood. Ours was a simple life, where a trip to Krauzer's Food Store for ice cream sandwiches was a cause for celebration.

But from an early age, I have never been someone who could let a simple thing go uncomplicated. Within days of opening a Christmas present containing a shiny new toy, I could be found dismantling said toy, eager to discover its inner workings. When *Scrabble* (and *Monopoly* and *Battleship*) got old, I invented my own board games with my own rules—to the eternal frustration of those unlucky enough to play them with me. Whereas other kids were content to simply enjoy the songs they heard on the radio, I had to know how they were made.

And so when I entered my teen years and fell feverishly in love with jazz and decided—with characteristic determination—that I was going to pursue a career as a jazz pianist, it didn't really take anyone by surprise. My parents were supportive, but they also feared that I wouldn't be able to support myself.

I auditioned for and got accepted to music school and eventually earned a diploma. I moved to New York City, where I lived in a basement apartment in Queens that flooded every time it rained, with a sweet older landlady who used to bring me bread, and I spent a couple years in grad school studying music composition, before unceremoniously dropping out. Ten years out of high school, when most of my peers had already shacked up with their childhood sweethearts and bought houses not far from home, I was a twenty-seven-year-old with no career prospects and a hundred thousand dollars in debt. I was barely earning enough money to cover rent and had to claim hardship to defer payment on my outstanding student loans.

Then everything changed for me. Not all at once and not conspicuously, but gradually, beginning with a single video performance I recorded at home and put on the Internet, just for kicks. The video went viral, and suddenly, I was inspired again. I began making more videos that combined my love of "vintage" styles of music with modern pop culture and invited my artistically inclined friends to join me in them. I had no idea where this new pastime might lead, or if it even would lead anywhere at all, but I knew that I enjoyed doing it and that viewers seemed to enjoy watching me do it, too. It wasn't long before I'd racked up a few more viral hits and light press coverage; then requests for interviews began rolling in.

In a couple of years, ScottBradleeLovesYa—the YouTube channel I'd launched to house these videos—grew from one subscriber (thanks, Mom!), to a thousand subscribers, to ten thousand subscribers, to one hundred thousand subscribers. Eventually, those online subscribers turned into something more tangible: I started to actually make money from them. I upgraded to a nicer, non-basement apartment (sans sweet landlady, sadly), and got invited to appear on national TV. I kept making those videos.

When my channel passed a million subscribers, I changed its name to better reflect the project it housed. (Branding, like everything else about being an entrepreneur, was something I learned on the job, through trial and error.) I put together a live musical act based on the channel, and we played our first tour of small clubs outside New York City, selling out every show. We toured Europe for two weeks. I moved to Los Angeles and arranged a residency for the group at a local nightclub, which continued to run even while we toured. I was offered multiple record deals but turned them all down to stay independent and went on to release seven albums in a single year on my own label. I kept on making those videos.

I brought on more performers and established a small touring company, which saw us playing gigs in venues twice as big across the United States, Europe, Australia, New Zealand, and Southeast Asia. Those venue sizes doubled again the next year. Along the way, we helped launch the careers of many talented performers, earning us the reputation of being "*Saturday Night Live* for singers."

By 2016, our roster of performers had blossomed into a full-fledged artistic community. We sent multiple casts on the road, simultaneously—an unprecedented feat for a concert act. I bought a very large house in Los Angeles to serve as the headquarters of the project…where, yes, I continued making those videos.

Later that year, I found myself near Times Square, watching a longtime dream come true. There, on the marquee of Radio City Music Hall, just a couple miles from the basement in which the project was originally hatched, were my name and that of the group I'd created. It was, to put it simply, surreal. I visited my old landlady and invited her to the show. She declined but asked if I could play the piano for her Christmas party.

This is the story of just how my life changed and how an improbably crazy idea grew to become a grassroots, global phenomenon. This is the story of Postmodern Jukebox.

MY FIRST GIG, OR HOW I GOT FIRED FROM WALMART

A ttention, Walmart shoppers: Come to the paint counter and get your groove on as we present the sweet sounds of Scott Bradlee and his Intergalactic Purveyors of Funk."

Long before the sold-out tour dates around the world, before the hundreds of millions of YouTube views, and before all my wildest dreams actually came true, this was how I announced my first public appearance as a bandleader: over the loudspeaker at the Walmart at which I worked. It wasn't exactly well-received, either; instead, it got me fired.

The Walmart in Clinton, New Jersey, was a logical place of employment for me in high school, mainly because it was the only place that was interested in hiring a very unskilled seventeen-year-old kid. It also happened to be the workplace of one of my best high school friends and fellow ne'er-do-wells, Cody (who, notoriously, would be fired not long after I started for making price tags that read "MY HAIRY ASS—$1.00" and slapping them on items around the store). In the brief, blissful time that our shifts overlapped, before Cody met his fate, we spent most of our on-the-job hours goofing off and talking music. On one particular afternoon, I had the idea to take things to the next level and actually *perform* music instead of merely sitting around talking about it.

I won't claim to have thought, at the time, that bringing in a live band to perform at the paint counter would result in anything other than my termination as a Walmart employee, but I do know this: Even then, the idea of putting music where it didn't belong fascinated me enough to throw caution and my Walmart career to the wind, just to see what would happen. The musicians who accompanied me—Cody on bass, Steve Ujfalussy on sax, and my friend Josh on conga drums—knew the drill; after all, I'd talked them into performing for confused customers at a gas station convenience store the previous week.

Upon arriving at the megastore that day, I channeled my inner James Bond and hijacked a large dolly, so as to wheel in my 1978 Fender Rhodes electric piano and a battery-powered amp in the smoothest, least obtrusive, least suspicion-stirring way possible. Realistic? Not at all. But it's the strategy I'd landed on, and I was committed to seeing it through. I pushed the array of instruments down the frozen food aisle, conscious, of course, of the weird glances I was receiving from customers. But there was no backing out now. This was my musical debut for the entire world, and the number one rule in showbiz is that *the show must go on*. With steely resolve, I executed a wide left turn into my usual station at the hardware department. With the help of my friends, I quickly set up the instruments around the paint counter before taking my place at the piano. Then, over the public-address system, I made the announcement that begins this tale.

The set began with a favorite of mine: Sly and the Family Stone's "If You Want Me to Stay." If nothing else, Walmart's customers seemed mildly entertained by this departure from the paint counter's usual programming, which consisted of my mixing paint for them and occasionally supergluing objects to the countertop out of boredom. A few even nodded their heads to the beat. It wasn't enough people to qualify as a crowd, exactly, but it was enough for me. I imagined myself onstage somewhere grand, with throngs of screaming fans cheering my every note.

A minute or so into the song, as I was passionately digging into the keys and wiping beads of sweat from my brow, I looked up to take in the sweep of my adoring fans only to find, instead, a formation of managers descending on us in a classic pincer movement. I snapped back to reality and stopped playing. A wave of discomfort washed over me as they arrived. My boss spoke.

"Scott, what are you doing?"

I felt it should have been obvious, but I figured I'd give him the benefit of the doubt and reply; he was my superior, after all.

"Playing a concert with my Intergalactic Purveyors of Funk, sir."

The requisite blank stare.

"You think this is a joke?"

There was no discussion about the artistic merit of what I was doing. I was fired on the spot, made to turn over my badge, and ordered to leave the store immediately. I complied, though not before belting out one last battle cry of rebellion with the band: a performance of Bob Marley's "Redemption Song," in protest, right outside the store's entrance, until the police were called. So ended my first show—and my last day of working for corporate America.

I wasn't troubled by this in the least. As I sat in my parents' driveway, trying to figure out how to explain my latest predicament to them in a way that might provoke some sympathy, I found my thoughts drifting to visions of someday getting the opportunity to tell this very story in front of a live audience. That'd show those managers the mistake they'd made, I thought. And in my rebellious teenage mind, anything seemed possible.

HOW TO SKIP YOUR
LESSONS AND STILL
BECOME A MUSICIAN

"24 minutes. 32 minutes. 28 minutes. 16 minutes. 29 minutes."
I was in the back seat of a silver Toyota Camry driven by my mother, a spiral-bound notebook splayed open in front of me. In it, I was furiously writing down my practice times for the previous week, meticulously alternating between using pen and pencil for entries. I wanted to create the illusion that I filled in my practice log daily and accurately, not arbitrarily and all at once on the ride over to my piano teacher's house. Truthfully, the amount of time I spent practicing piano each day of the previous week was quite easy to remember—because I never practiced the piano.

That I never practiced the piano was no secret to my teacher; I was a terrible liar, especially for an eleven-year-old who probably had a lot of things to lie about and, as such, had just as many opportunities to hone his lying skills. Every week, she would put the same Clementi sonatina in front of me on her cherry upright piano in her immaculately maintained parlor room, and I would do my best to pretend that I had spent hours practicing each section on my parents' spinet piano. Every week, I would express faux frustration at my predicament.

"I practiced this part so much last week....I don't know why I can't get it to sound right! Maybe I'm just not *able* to learn piano."

My teacher was too gentle to call me out on my lies, but on this particular day, as she demonstrated how the section I'd been assigned for the past three weeks was supposed to sound, she looked more dispassionate than usual. That's because she'd already decided that this was the last lesson I would be taking from her. Suffice it to say, it was a decision that improved both our lives.

In retrospect, I'm able to clearly see that formal lessons were never going to work for me—for two reasons. First, I loathed being forced to do anything I didn't want to, and the lessons always felt like something I was enduring to appease my parents. And second, as I realized much later on, what appealed to me so much about music, in general, was its potential for *rebellion*—the fact that you could elicit a range of emotions, from bemusement to shock, in an audience, merely by playing something unexpected. In the drudgery of the Czerny and Hanon exercises that I was learning, there didn't seem to be any space for that sort of magic.

That I allowed my parents to waste their money on lessons I wasn't committed to is something that I still feel pangs of remorse about all these years later. They were too generous and sweet to deserve that, and although we were by no means poor, we also weren't wealthy. Born to a blue-collar family and raised in Brooklyn, my mother, Sunday, was a Spanish teacher at Amityville High School. She played violin and sang in college, and to this day she still picks out songs on the guitar that she learned to play during a year abroad in Madrid. My father, Richard, a computer programmer, was raised by a single mother in Providence, Rhode Island, and grew up to be the honest, loyal father that he never had. My parents had been married five years when I was born, but they were still finding their footing in their careers. Through sacrifice and a few years of diligent saving, they were able to scrape together enough for a down payment on a plot of land in an undeveloped neighborhood in central New Jersey, away from the hustle and bustle of New York City. They wasted no time getting down to building the small, contemporary-style home they'd envisioned for their family, and in many of my photographic appearances as a five-year-old, I'm wearing OshKosh overalls and a painter's cap, attempting to help apply a layer of primer on the interior. I wasn't much help, but I *was* cheap labor, requiring little more than an arrowroot biscuit and an Ocean Spray juice box for compensation. The home they built for us— first, for just we three, and then, too, for my sister, Mollie, who came along seven years after me—was a happy and loving one. We may have spent an initial few years without proper flooring or heating, but in terms of growing up with a stable family life, I was indeed very, very fortunate.

For my sixth birthday, my parents bought me my first vinyl record (keep in mind this was the preferred medium at the time; Sunday and Richard were not hipsters): Michael Jackson's *Bad*. To say I was obsessed with this record is an understatement. I learned how to operate the turntable just so I could listen to "Smooth Criminal" on repeat, however many times I wanted, whenever I wanted. Michael Jackson provided the soundtrack for my own private performances of the moonwalk, which, at six years of age, entailed simply walking backward. I learned to read by poring over the lyrics insert, matching the words to what Michael was singing, which on one unforgettable occasion led to my poor mother having to define "seduce" for me in the most

G-rated manner possible. For the rest of the year, that album and Paul Simon's *Graceland* were on constant rotation in our house. In first grade, I insisted on singing "Man in the Mirror" in the school talent show. (I couldn't pronounce my *r*'s back then, so it actually came out more like "Man in the Miwwow.") I'm lucky to have the audio of that very first public performance preserved for posterity; my parents proudly captured it with their brand-new tape recorder.

I had a lot of interests when I entered middle school, but music wasn't necessarily at the top of the list. I loved baseball and enjoyed collecting baseball cards (although I was never brave enough to try the stale pieces of gum that—inexplicably to me—accompanied the packs of said cards). I enjoyed building things but even more so enjoyed taking things apart to try to discover how they worked. It was fairly typical of me to hound my parents for months to buy me an electronic game of some sort and then, within hours of receiving it, for me to render it inoperable by disassembling it and rearranging the microchips in a different order.

My musical tastes at that point in time were largely dictated by my friend Steve Rekuc from down the road, who was a couple years older and infinitely cooler than me—which was at least partially owed to his house having a pool and cable TV. Under Steve's tutelage, I developed an affinity for MTV and *The Fresh Prince of Bel-Air*, and I made my first cassette purchase wisely: *Please Hammer, Don't Hurt 'Em* by MC Hammer. We would listen to hits like "Can't Touch This" while we shot hoops and played video games, and I took dressing in corresponding attire very seriously. From ages eight to eleven, I almost exclusively wore some combination of Ocean Pacific beachwear, baggy pants with loud designs (called "skids"), and a rotating selection of fluorescent hats. In the annual bus stop back-to-school picture, I was the kid taking fashion cues from *Sinbad*.

I was nine when the era of my formal piano lessons began, though it didn't take long for my parents to realize where piano fell on my list of priorities: extremely low. Piano lessons, as it turns out, typically aren't the most exciting activity for a young kid from rural New Jersey who dresses like Sinbad and listens to C+C Music Factory. The summer before I entered fifth grade, my piano teacher conveniently went away on an extended vacation, and when she returned, before my mom even had a chance to inquire, was quick to notify us that she'd managed already to fill her entire schedule for the coming semester. And with that, my short-lived classical piano career came to a grinding halt. I was overjoyed.

I'm of the opinion that the very first step in learning any discipline is finding a way to get yourself feeling profoundly inspired and invested. Learning to master a skill is a long, arduous process, involving many stagnant plateaus and discouraging disappointments. Unless you're approaching your learning from a place of genuine inspiration, you're probably going to have a hard time staying committed to the process, especially when the going gets tough. Motivation alone can sustain you—but only for so long; psyching yourself up to do something you don't *really want* to do gets old, fast. For me, it was the stiff nature of the lessons that blocked my pathways to inspiration and turned practicing into a chore.

It wasn't my teacher's fault that, at age eleven, I possessed neither the inspiration nor motivation to learn piano; I simply wasn't enamored with classical music or the thought of being a pianist in general. My mom, used to dealing with all sorts of stubborn children as a teacher, accepted this in stride with her usual optimism.

"I do think you'll come to see how much enjoyment music can bring you. Maybe you'll return to piano someday," she offered hopefully.

"Fat chance," I scoffed, *profoundly inspired* at the time by the sardonic wit of my beloved *Calvin and Hobbes* comic books.

Despite being a quitter when it came to piano, I was a pretty observant and studious child and definitely very curious about the world—a trait that my mom, in particular, encouraged. In school, I placed great emphasis on learning as much as I could, to the point where I spent first-grade math class quietly working out of a folder of more advanced work in the back corner of the room...by choice. My hope of being the smartest kid in the world was all but shattered a month later, when I glanced up from yet another set of boring division problems and saw, across the room, the rest of the class being plied with M&M's into performing basic addition and subtraction problems, ostensibly to conflate the dubious joys of math with the verifiable joys of sugar consumption. And so it was that, at the ripe old age of seven, I became enlightened to the fact that this world we live in is not just and that organized education breeds disillusionment for some. My piano teacher never stood a chance. If I was to learn the instrument, it would have to be on my own terms.

I first heard the piece of music that would change my life when a next-door neighbor—a more advanced and much more diligent piano student than I was—began studying George Gershwin's *Rhapsody in Blue*. Exciting, humorous, brash, and alive and adult, it sounded nothing like any piano piece I'd heard before—nothing like the stuffy sonatinas that I had been assigned (nothing against sonatinas, of course), and it got under my skin. It got me wondering whether maybe, just maybe, I hadn't given piano enough of a shot.

It had been a year since my last piano lesson, and when I wasn't busy collecting cassettes of music that spoke to me—the rap duo Kris Kross was now the artist *du jour*—I began dabbling in attempts to pick up where I'd left off with piano—on my own.

Coming into adolescence, I decided to abandon my previously held career aspirations—astronaut, professional baseball player, and cartoonist—and rebrand myself as a talented pianist, setting out to teach myself pieces that would impress and captivate my hypothetical audience. These pieces, as you likely could have guessed, tended to be far beyond my skill level: "Puck" by Grieg, Liszt's "Hungarian Rhapsody #2," and Chopin's "Polonaise in A Major." Although I lacked the technique to play them well, I was able to sort of stumble through the sheet music through brute force, and gradually, my skill level increased. More importantly, though, I was *enjoying* the challenge, often spending three or four hours in a single day tackling difficult passages.

Through it all, *Rhapsody in Blue* was in the back of my mind—as my end goal, as my reward for all this training. And not the abridged version that my neighbor played; I wanted to play the real-deal version that Leonard Bernstein recorded. I spent weeks calling every music store in a fifty-mile radius, attempting to track down that original, unabridged version. In that pre-Internet era, I often asked the disinterested store clerks to thumb through the pages and describe to me over the phone the way the notes looked on the page. Finally, I hit upon success, and my dad drove all the way to Princeton to retrieve the piece of music that I had long dreamed of playing. He had the sheet music waiting for me in a tan sleeve when I got home from school that glorious afternoon. Holding my breath, I nervously turned past the blue cover to see if it was, indeed, the complete version. The opening page was full of elegant *glissandos* and complex notation; *this was it.* I thanked my dad for heroically going well out of his way to make this possible and then wasted no time in tearing into the music on our old spinet piano with the sticking keys. I remember, in the moment, thinking to myself that it was a day I'd never forget. That's proved true, but it ended up being more than unforgettable: It would go down in my personal history as a life-changing day, as well.

Rhapsody in Blue was hard. Really hard. It didn't take me long to figure out that the sheet music I had in my possession was actually the piano *reduction,* meaning that it wasn't solely the piano part of the orchestral score that I heard Leonard Bernstein play but the entire score for all instruments, just kind of mashed together into two staves. Some passages seemed to require a third hand. Undaunted, I tore into the score in the same way that I read books: I skipped right on ahead to the interesting parts first.

At the time, the "interesting" parts, to me, were the jazz-influenced bits: the piano runs and chromatic passages; the iconic, blue note–heavy theme; the slow, bluesy riff that led to the memorable United Airlines commercial jingle (sorry, Gershwin). I would pick apart these exotic, intriguing passages, trying to unearth their inner workings the same way I had taken apart my toys a few years earlier. A whole new world opened up for me when, in an attempt to find other pieces with the sounds I so loved, I started looking into Gershwin's non-classical influences. I decided that I needed to explore this thing called *ragtime piano,* and I hungrily read about its history and practitioners as I worked my way through a book of Scott Joplin piano rags. Inspiration, it seemed, was taking me to new places that the structured tutorials of an expert never had.

My journey took me far and wide and nearly a century back in time. I learned about *stride piano*—a kind of fancier version of ragtime—and listened in awe as Fats Waller played "A Handful of Keys." I couldn't find any sheet music for this one, but thanks to the Joplin book, I had a pretty solid training on the *oom-pah* left-hand and standard ragtime chords, and I managed to pick out a good chunk of it by ear. I learned about how *diminished* chords were used in jazz and how to roll octaves to create a

11

tremolo effect. I devoured books about the birth of jazz in New Orleans and its key figures: Jelly Roll Morton, Louis Armstrong, Bix Beiderbecke. I took out CDs and cassettes by the dozen from my local library and would sit at the piano with headphones on, rewinding passages again and again and trying to mimic them. My repertoire grew: "Carolina Shout" by James P. Johnson, "Black and Tan Fantasy" by Duke Ellington, "The Pearls" by Jelly Roll Morton. The hours flew by; there weren't enough in the day to sate my need to play and learn and explore. Suddenly, the instrument my parents couldn't have bribed me to go near in the not-so-distant past had become my most favorite companion and the source of much joy.

The piano, for me, was a portal to another universe: a place of dimly lit nightclubs with dancing flappers, lively *second-line* New Orleans parades, and larger-than-life music legends competing with one another for glory. I imagined performing with my own jazz band at raucous parties and meeting all the colorful characters congregated therein. When I played, I felt a connection with all the legendary performers who created this music; even in 1995, a James P. Johnson lick still sounded exactly as it would have sounded at the moment of conception. It was as though I had found a way to slip through the fabric of time and place myself smack-dab into a bygone era. Playing jazz helped me find a place where I belonged—even if it mostly existed in my mind. For a skinny kid in New Jersey, with braces, a greasy bowl cut, and questionable taste in fashion, this other universe offered a welcome escape from the growing pains of the real world, and in the hours I wasn't there, it was the only place I dreamt of being.

FALLING IN LOVE
WITH THE PROCESS

To the amazement of my parents—and to my *own* amazement—practicing the piano was no longer something I fought against tooth and nail. Instead, knowing that I wanted to be a piano player, and knowing that practicing, of course, was just *something piano players did*, I turned my daily practice into a *habit*. Now, habits get a bad rap; we tend to think of things like biting our nails or smoking when we talk about them. But really, a habit is defined as "a settled or regular tendency or practice, especially one that is hard to give up." Tooth brushing is a habit (for most of us). So is showing up to work on time. Those are some good habits. Habits can be good; say it with me.

Once you've trained your brain to view practicing as a habit, the next step is finding the *motivation* to adopt that habit. The key to motivation, I've learned, is coupling your profound inspiration to a strong belief in yourself, and that's not something even the best teacher is able to instill. It has to come from within. Building a strong core identity to drive your motivation requires first believing that you'll eventually master the skill you've set out to learn—no matter how farfetched that might initially seem to yourself and others. Having the correct image of yourself is really key here; you have to think of yourself as the thing you want to be long before other people think of you as that. You may only have taken one trumpet lesson and sound horrible, but you still must think of yourself as a trumpet player in order for the habit to stick. You are whatever you do repeatedly.

Practicing became such a constant in my day—and in such a natural, unforced way—that I hardly had to think about it. It had become, in other words, a habit. Progress came very quickly, and the bulk of my piano skill was developed between the ages of twelve and fourteen; after that, it was for the most part a matter of refining the rough edges of my homegrown technique and learning the theory behind the pieces I played. I lived and breathed jazz piano in those years, to the exclusion of everything else. School was still a drag for me, and I'd begun to channel the profound inspiration I drew from *Calvin and Hobbes* into pulling pranks on my teachers to create disruptions in class. These pranks ranged from drawing caricatures of my teachers in a variety of embarrassing contexts and completing my math homework in the style and format of a Publisher's Clearinghouse sweepstakes letter, to attending seventh-grade classes for a week straight, which wouldn't have been a problem except for the fact that I was in eighth grade. My mom, always quick to defend her beloved progeny, was of little use to the teachers who called our house to complain.

"Oh, he's so creative, isn't he?" she would beam, blissfully ignorant of my less-than-angelic behavior at school and stubbornly resistant to being enlightened about it.

My antics garnered me a lot of attention and occasionally praise from classmates, but in actuality, I was something of a loner in junior high. I had only a few friends, and they tended to be the other troublemakers I occasionally enlisted in my campaigns of mischief. I was largely all right with this, preferring to race home right after school to practice piano anyway, rather than hang around and try to fit in.

By the time high school started, others had finally begun to see me as I saw myself: as a talented pianist, a "music kid." I made friends with a group of misfits and musicians who shared my distaste for the rigidity of school and our homogenous, boring small town, as idyllic as it was. They were outsiders and proud of it; they smoked weed, caused trouble, and were generally disliked by the more popular kids in school. I was definitely the straight edge in the bunch, but as a quiet teenager with very few friends, I was grateful to find a group that accepted me. One of our crew, Cody (of Walmart story fame), lived near the high school; we'd often all cut class to jam on instruments at his house. I showed my new friends the style of jazz that I was into, and although it wasn't really their speed, they appreciated my talent and always talked me up to the people we encountered. Or at least, they tried to:

CUTE GIRL AT A PARTY: Hi.

ME: Hi, I'm Scott. So, um...cool party, huh?

FRIEND: Scott's a *huge pianist*.

CUTE GIRL: Excuse me?

ME: (frantically pantomiming playing the piano, trying to rescue the situation) He means "piano player"; I'm a piano player.

FRIEND: Yeah, a really big one. Like a really big pianist. You should date him!

CUTE GIRL: ...I'm just going to leave now. Nice meeting you two.

I may not have been confident socializing with the opposite sex, but I was becoming very confident in my skills as a musician. There's an inherent contradiction embedded in practice—at least that I've found in my experience: While motivation to put in the hours comes from being confident in your ability to eventually master and contribute to a craft, *arriving* at that confidence to begin with often requires putting in many, many hours of practice. This catch-22 is the reason so many people pick up the guitar only to quit after learning a couple Jimmy Buffett songs—it's difficult to imagine yourself as anything but a beginner when you are starting out.

After several years of consistent practice, I was beginning to discover what I could contribute to the lexicon of jazz. Thanks to my friends and their tastes, I developed an appreciation for non-jazz styles of music, too. Initially, this meant gangsta rap by hip-hop artists like Notorious B.I.G., 2Pac, and Dr. Dre—all artists who frequently sampled jazz and soul licks in their instrumentals. I enjoyed picking out those references to older songs and styles and seeing how artists paid homage to music's colorful history. At home, I began to play hip-hop mixtapes over my speakers while improvising on the piano at the same time; suddenly, the repetitive instrumentals became *modal jazz,* the laid-back, cool style of jazz pioneered by Miles Davis on his bestselling album *Kind of Blue.* The possibilities of somehow updating my musical vocabulary by filtering it through more current or popular genres of music fascinated me.

One day, while hanging out with some friends at my house, I made the bold claim that I could turn any song into a jazz song.

"Name any rap song," I boasted, "and I'll make it into jazz."

"*Any* song? You mean, any song with a piano part, right?"

"No, I mean *any* song," I corrected. "Trust me, I can do it."

"Okay, how about some Biggie? Play 'Big Poppa.'"

Easy; the Notorious B.I.G. track sampled an already jazzy Isley Brothers song, "Between the Sheets." I played it as jazz by swinging the synth line, giving it a Count Basie feel. After finishing, I further demonstrated my ability by playing it with a stride left hard, giving it a turn-of-the-century ragtime feel. Now I was just showing off, but I couldn't help it. This was exciting for me, too. It took my friends a beat to wrap their heads around the transformed tune, but once they had done so, they were roaring with delight.

"That's crazy!! I could actually *hear* the song in there. Do another one—what about some Weezer?"

I obliged, spending the next hour turning contemporary hits by groups like Sublime and Red Hot Chili Peppers into jazz and ragtime songs. It was fun watching my friends' faces as they recognized each one. But most satisfying of all for me was that they were enjoying the vintage sounds, despite having always professed not to enjoy jazz. This was progress.

Just as I was helping my friends appreciate music from a half-century before, so, too, were they helping me develop a genuine interest in the songs released in the past few years. It was a win–win situation. One song that I particularly connected with was Radiohead's first and biggest hit, the grunge-inspired anthem "Creep." It spoke to me, its chorus pretty much summing up my high school experience with effortless ease:

But I'm a creep, I'm a weirdo.
What the hell am I doing here?
I don't belong here....

"Creep" reminded me of being a freshman and going to a school dance for the first time. I was painfully shy and completely out of my element, a scrawny kid in a setting populated by older, self-assured jocks and cheerleaders breezily joking around and flirting with one another. When I arrived, I spent a good thirty minutes scanning the room, looking for someone—anyone—that I recognized, before giving up. Defeated, I traipsed outside and sat on the curb until my dad came to get me a couple hours later. It's not exactly a memory I like recalling, but I loved the chords in that song. They sounded a bit like the old jazz standard "On the Sunny Side of the Street," and every once in a while, I would find myself noodling around on the piano, improvising over them.

My musical ability developed in tandem with my expanding love for the breadth of musical genres, and my focus became understanding each genre's discrete elements, breaking them down and reassembling them, putting them in contact in ways I'd never heard before. Instead of doing my homework in high school, I continued exploring the link between hip-hop and jazz, eventually discovering jazz-influenced groups like A Tribe Called Quest and De La Soul. From there I fell further down the rabbit hole, arriving at the source of so many of their instrumental samples: '70s funk like Parliament-Funkadelic, James Brown, Stevie Wonder, and Ohio Players. This was party music, no doubt about it, but at its core it still possessed the organic essence of improvised music that attracted me to jazz.

As a pianist, jazz was my first love—that would never change—but bit by bit I was learning that there were jazz roots in everything I was listening to and that playing one genre didn't mean that I couldn't play other genres, too. It was an exciting realization for me, a realization in no small part indebted to my "party trick" of turning pop songs into jazz. Like most other people, I'd taken genres for granted as something akin to rigid boxes with established rules, but really, I was discovering, they are more like streams, meandering and converging as they wind their way to a river; the water flows freely, and it is impossible to say for sure where a new stream begins and an old one continues with the added force of a tributary. I decided that calling myself a "jazz pianist" was too limiting. I would be a "jazz pianist who also performed funk and hip-hop." It was a specific niche I'd carved out for myself but one that I soon found a home for, on the Internet.

CREATING THE FUTURE
BY EMBRACING THE PAST

E ven as I was enamored, primarily, with musical history, I enjoyed experimenting with new sounds, too. At my occasional live performance—I had been repurposed as a pianist at a deli after the manager discovered my short-order cooking skills to be seriously lacking—I was getting a better response to my era-collapsing mashups than anything I'd played before. By embracing the sounds that were most familiar to people, I was able to connect with them and get them to trust me as their guide through the uncharted territory of "vintage music."

Through it all, though, jazz remained my calling. On my bedroom wall I hung a reproduction of Art Kane's legendary 1958 photograph "A Great Day in Harlem," given to me by my aunt and uncle. The photograph, which showed fifty-seven famous jazz musicians gathered in front of a brownstone in Harlem, endlessly fascinated me. Each night before I went to sleep I studied it, noticing different details. There's Count Basie, sitting on the curb because he'd grown tired of standing. Above him is Thelonious Monk, wearing shades and a light-colored jacket, perhaps to be more conspicuous. Off near the fringes, clad in his trademark porkpie hat and with his body facing slightly away from the camera, was Lester Young. I imagined the stories behind the assembly of such an awesome collection of talent in one place. All fifty-seven of them had dedicated their lives to contributing to jazz, America's first truly original art form. It was awe-inspiring to imagine the dedication they possessed.

Occasional trips into New York City soon became a reliable source of inspiration for me as a teenager. My outsider friends and I were bored of being confined to the parameters of our small, conventional town and dreamed of the day that we would experience freedom from the monotony and oppression of high school. Taking the train into Penn Station on a Saturday offered us a glimmer of that someday freedom. We made the most of every second there—sifting through vinyl at record stores, watching drum circles and chess matches at Union Square, and sneaking into bars to hear live music. By the time we caught the last train on the Raritan Valley line home, we'd be feeling physically exhausted but mentally energized. Even to this day, no experience surpasses the excitement and optimism I feel stepping outside the station and seeing the lights of New York City dance in the night, the wind whipping around the Midtown high-rises.

Back home, I finished out my high school career with a flourish, graduating in the bottom half of my class of three hundred. My parents, unsurprisingly, were horrified; even my perennially positive mother couldn't manage to find a positive spin for this achievement.

"I'm not angry with you; I'm *disappointed* in you," she intoned sternly, placing my report card before me on the dining room table, where I sat with downcast eyes.

This just feels awful, I remember thinking. I would've preferred her to be angry.

As much as I hated school, as much as I struggled through my classes until eventually succumbing to the tides of mediocrity and no longer trying, I wanted my parents to be proud of me. They were both first-generation college graduates, and they'd worked so hard to give me and my sister every advantage throughout our childhoods. I felt ashamed and wished I could somehow go back in time and redo my schooling with greater effort and focus; I would have done so in a heartbeat, knowing how much it meant to my parents. But hindsight is 20/20, and sitting there then, met with my mother's sadness, I found myself silently vowing to give my all—from that moment on—to realizing my musical dreams and achieving success as a musician, no matter how tough it got. My grades may have fallen short of my parents' expectations for me, but I knew I could still do them proud with other accomplishments in life.

AN UNDERACHIEVER'S GUIDE TO FUMBLING THROUGH HIGHER EDUCATION

Graduating high school in the bottom half of my class wasn't exactly the strongest indicator that I would meet with any more success in college. My abysmal showing in both the humanities and sciences did, however, all but cement the idea that, if my educational journey were to continue, it was going to involve a pursuit of the arts. To get accepted to any decent college, you see, I would have to apply with a declared major in music. Obviously, this sounded far from the worst fate to me, and the range of schools it opened up for consideration— from conservatories like the Eastman School of Music at the University of Rochester and Berklee College of Music in Boston, to general universities like Rowan University and SUNY Purchase, which also had jazz programs—was enticing and wide. Ultimately, I wound up selecting The Hartt School at University of Hartford, which seemed to be the best of both worlds: a conservatory within a university. On top of my excitement about its program offerings, it also was the school that offered me the most substantial scholarship, which helped make up for its tuition being a bit higher than what my family could afford.

A WARNING TO MY FELLOW MUSIC KIDS

I want to take a second here to talk about my decision to go to school for music, since I get asked for advice on this pretty often. If you're a young musician (or dancer, or musical theatre actor, or any type of creative performer for that matter) and you've progressed in your abilities to the point that a career in the arts seems like a viable path forward, it's only logical that you'll find yourself considering a formal continuation of your music studies post–high school. Whether you go the route of the conservatory or enroll in a music program within a more traditional college, you'll receive training from professional musicians, perform in ensembles alongside other talented students, and have access to state-of-the-art facilities and concert halls. The icing on the cake? You'll get to sleep in late on weekdays, take classes that appeal to you, and surround yourself with artsy, inspiring kids who share your interests and passions. If all that sounds like a dream, it's because, in many ways, it is. But any dream has its potential downsides, and I think that it's important that you're aware of them, too.

It's no secret that colleges in the United States—in particular, the private schools that host many of the top music programs—are expensive. *Seriously* expensive. Colleges are big businesses, and, like any other business, they're driven by profit goals. While some of your professors will be genuinely caring, helpful, and enthusiastic about imparting knowledge, others will, undoubtedly, be motivated to teach, in large part, by their desire to collect a steady paycheck.

You may also find that the real-world career counseling

available to you in music school is severely lacking, especially compared to the counseling at other majors' disposal, since the usual rules of job placement just don't apply to musicians. Now, I'm not saying that spending forty thousand dollars a year to study in a conservatory is a waste of money, necessarily—only that you should keep in mind that no school or degree can guarantee that a career in your chosen field awaits you on the other side. Do your research—and that includes talking to current students and alumni—before enrolling in any program.

This is extra crucial if you're planning to take out significant student loans to pay for said schooling. As we will see, I can tell you firsthand that financial decisions have a way of following you around for *years*.

To me, the true value of college is not in *what* you learn but in *how you go about* learning. Essential, for instance, is keeping yourself open to experiencing unexpected insights, even if they conflict with previously held views. That mind-set will serve you well in school, though really, it's a mind-set worth striving for throughout *all* of life. At the end of first semester, I wound up surprising my parents with straight A's, which they joyously celebrated as a sign that I'd finally gotten my act together. I hadn't, exactly, but I *was* learning—just not in the conventional sense. Yes, I still cut class on occasion; yes, I still neglected to do a fair number of my assignments; and yes, I still often went out partying instead of studying. These behaviors were somewhat expected of jazz studies majors, though, and most of our teachers made it clear from the get-go that they didn't believe in grades anyway.

What's most important, though, is that I entered Hartt with a hunger to unleash and hone my talent as a musician, and I was prepared to do that by making the most of every possible resource available to me, both in and outside the classroom.

24

From day one I treated the campus as my laboratory, hosting jam sessions, putting together ambitious musical productions, and inviting musicians to lay down tracks in my dorm room-turned-recording studio. And of course, I still was preoccupied with pushing boundaries and egging on my friends to do ridiculous things—stealing signs, setting off fireworks, and throwing raucous parties that eventually got us evicted from campus housing in the first of many evictions I'd live to tell of. But gradually, I was realizing that boundary-pushing could be just as satisfying when it leads to creative innovation and personal growth as when it results in minor destruction.

In an unexpected twist, going to school specifically for jazz had, to a degree, cured me of my desire to focus *solely* on jazz. The fact that thirty or so other students in my year were studying exactly the same recordings rubbed me the wrong way, and I started looking for ways to stand out. I purposefully immersed myself in artists and genres I'd not explored much before, spending hours listening to their works and mapping out the characteristics. Certain works stuck out as particularly inspiring: *Abbey Road* by the Beatles for its form; *La Bohème* by Puccini for its beautiful melodies; and nearly the entirety of Elvis Costello's discography for its lyrical richness. Jazz, Motown, and soul remained my passions, but I was learning to appreciate non-jazz music a whole lot more alongside them.

As for modern-day pop, well, I couldn't say the same. I didn't dedicate my energies to disliking Top 40 radio so much as I tried to remain blissfully ignorant of it, with the exception of retro-themed hits like "Hey Ya!" by OutKast. Pop music, with its unsophisticated chord structures and inane lyrics, carried, for me, the connotation of lame fraternity parties and Hartford's generic, college-themed bars, and I wanted no part in either.

FINDING MY NICHE

By the end of the first year of college, I'd matured leaps and bounds, taking my schooling and myself ever more seriously...though that's not to say I didn't have a ways to go. My rebellious streak still stubbornly prevented me from believing I could enjoy playing in someone else's group. Sure, I enjoyed the performance opportunities that college afforded me, be they jazz ensemble classes or the occasional fill-in keyboard gig at a local bar (getting into a bar while underage was still very, very exciting to me), but I harbored serious dreams of leading a band.

In my sophomore year, I decided to try my hand at leading a four-piece group for the first time since my fateful farewell concert at Walmart. I had a good friend named Sesha Loop, and I thought her name would make for a cool band name. So, that's what I named the band: The Sesha Loop. Sesha didn't seem particularly bothered by this appropriation of her identity, but I'm not sure she realized just how seriously or far I was planning to take the whole endeavor. After snapping a cliché "indie rock" photo of the four of us wearing leather jackets in my messy dorm room, we were officially a band. Time to take the world by storm.

The Sesha Loop was my first attempt at a lot of things—songwriting, singing, booking gigs. As with any other new path being forged, there were bumps along the way. For starters, I didn't know how to sing, so I settled on (mostly poorly) shouting the esoteric, Britpop-inspired lyrics I'd written for the group while also playing piano and synth simultaneously. And then there was the matter of drums. Our drummer didn't have a real drum kit on campus, so he played instead on an electronic kit that lent the music an unintentional '80s vibe.

Thanks to some reckless credit card spending, I had acquired enough recording gear for us to make a four-song demo, which I poured my heart and soul into. I burned it onto CDs and sent it off to local music venues—along with our badass band photo, of course. That brazen self-promotion paid off in the form of our first gig at a pool hall in Middletown, Connecticut. To say that I spent hours mentally preparing for this triumphant debut would be an understatement.

While it may not come as a surprise to you, I was shocked to learn that no one at the pool hall that Tuesday night was there to hear the music. Call me overly optimistic, but this truth became evident to me only after we'd entered the venue and begun setting up our gear. The clientele was older than us—way older—and very much focused on sinking shots and drinking. We met the "sound guy," a very drunk man who accidentally burned my hand with his cigarette as he attempted to set up the mic. Small setbacks be damned, we persevered and tentatively started to play. Was I, in that moment, hoping that the room, upon hearing the siren sound of our music, would collectively abandon its pool cues and fall under a spell? Indeed, I was.

"Ladies and gentleman," I announced dramatically, "you are about to witness the *very first* performance of The Sesha Loop." I waited a few beats to allow for the applause.

It never came.

"They must not have heard me. Play a big drumroll," I

whisper-hissed to our drummer. An odd static-y '80s-sounding rumble emerged from the electronic set. I stared ahead blankly. Not being a drummer myself, I hadn't known that doing a roll on a cheap electronic set leaves something to be desired.

Well this is off to a great start, I thought.

The first song ended to no applause. In fact, there was no acknowledgment whatsoever from the room that there was even a band onstage. We burned through our forty-five minutes of material without so much as a blink from the crowd. At one point during the set, I started to take my pants off to see if I could get any kind of reaction from the preoccupied patrons we thought of as our "audience." Nope. Eleven rolled around, and the sound guy—who by now was exhibiting significant difficulty standing upright—paid us forty dollars for our efforts: a generous sum, considering the debatable entertainment value we'd provided.

All in all, it was a terrible gig, but I had an absolute blast. *If this earned us forty dollars, imagine what we could make if we landed a gig where people actually came to listen!*

Undeterred, perhaps even strangely encouraged, I kept booking shows for The Sesha Loop. We played venues as diverse as coffeehouses and skate parks. We started getting people to show up, listen, and—when they had been drinking heavily enough—even dance. I learned a little about live sound and mixing, and I became pretty skilled at talking to venue managers in a way that made it almost seem like I knew what I was talking about ("we need more 60 Hz in the bass!").

Something I actually *did* know about, however, was the importance of connecting with fans. With this sincere goal in mind, I bought a hardcover "yearbook" and filled it with random pictures of us and asked fans to write their email addresses along with made-up memories of us, as though we'd attended high school together. It was a silly gimmick, but it was effective.

Thanks to this yearbook, I slowly built a small mailing list, eventually growing it to the point where I could count on having at least a handful of people at every show.

Tiring of The Sesha Loop concept after a year or so, I put it into hiatus (to Sesha's relief) and rebranded our group as an even more bizarre project: a faux–British New Wave band called Gordon Hunter & The Wandering Rocks, fronted by none other than yours truly—with a British accent. My goal was to make us the most pretentious act in Hartford, and I'm pretty sure we succeeded. There were eight others in the band, in addition to my character Gordon, who channeled Morrissey vocally and a poor man's James Joyce lyrically. Among these were a second keyboardist who was only allowed to speak French and a girl who performed dramatic monologues—ostensibly written by Gordon—in between songs. It was quite the spectacle. Per my own rules, we remained in character throughout the night, even when faced with significant setbacks. On one occasion, the second keyboard malfunctioned while we were onstage, which resulted in a minor crisis that became something of an international incident:

GORDON: (in a poorly executed British accent) Bloody hell, Kate! What is the problem?

KATE: (quietly, off mic, in American English) The keyboard, it just turned off. I think it lost power?

GORDON: (over the mic, exaggeratedly) Kate! I know you *ONLY SPEAK FRENCH*, but tell me what's wrong, please!

KATE: (hesitating before obediently tapping into four years of high school French) *Le clavier est cassé.*

GORDON: [beat] For the love of—! Does anyone here speak French and can translate what she's saying?

We weren't well-known, even locally, but the people who stumbled upon our group were consistently amused by the onstage craziness, and I'd like to think that personal touch of craziness played some role in turning happenstance listeners into fans. When spectators complimented me on a job well done, "Gordon" responded with an egotistical "I know," delivered in a crudely attempted London dialect. Being in character as Gordon allowed me to act truly obnoxious without having it reflect poorly on me; it was too much fun.

While my collegiate creative pursuits could never be considered "successful" by any conventional measure, they did offer me ample opportunity to experiment, explore, and nurture my musical identities. Crucially, too, they encouraged me to bring other musicians into the mix. It was no longer just my piano and me; I now had access to a network of talented musicians who could make sounds that I couldn't make on my own. It was my first taste of the magic of collaboration, which would one day lead me to fantastic new places.

HOW TO PAY YOUR BILLS
DOING SOMETHING
YOU KIND OF ENJOY

L et's start with the bad news: When you take off the training wheels and get out into the workforce for the very first time, you are probably *not* going to be doing what you love. It's a bummer, but the world doesn't owe you this, and that's not going to change just because you're talented or graduated as the valedictorian of your class. The good news is that it *is* possible to find employment that, while it may not fill your eyes with stars, also won't eat away at your soul entirely. As a creative person, landing a job of this caliber—and one that ideally leaves you with some spare time to hone your craft—should be your goal. None of your creative dreams can come true if you're not able to pay your bills.

Speaking of paying the bills...that's a learning process in and of itself. And if you're anything like me, it might take suffering the consequences of *not* paying them a few times before the lesson is properly instilled. In 2005, after I graduated from the University of Hartford (as a "five-year plan" student; I was still an underachiever), I spent the following year living in a house that I rented with four college friends in what became something

31

of an extension of college life. We succeeded in getting evicted not once but twice, for falling significantly behind on our rent payments. Not that it's any excuse, but we were all in our early twenties, with absolutely no financial wherewithal. The following conversation, which I distinctly remember having with one of the housemates, Hobbes, pretty much sums it up:

HOBBES: (answers flip phone) Hello? (closes flip phone abruptly)

ME: Who was that?

HOBBES: It was that collection agency again. I owe them, like, two grand.

ME: Shouldn't you pay that?

HOBBES: Nah, dude. Do you know what happens to those bills if they can't get in touch with you? They just disappear, dude.

ME: Really?

HOBBES: Yeah man, they just give up. They can't force you to pay. It's the biggest loophole in the credit system.

Indeed, our household was hell-bent on exploiting this supposed "loophole." I surfed credit cards to outfit a home studio top to bottom with music gear, amassing over five thousand dollars of high-interest credit card debt, which I then quickly defaulted on by adhering to our game plan of not answering the phone. Our gas was shut off periodically because our bills went unpaid for months. Even our debts to one another were treated with the same haphazard, illogical care; at one point, the fifty dollars that one roommate owed me somehow became the responsibility of a different roommate. It was complete madness, and yet we did nothing to stop it for a good long while.

It was only when our fiscal shenanigans resulted in a second eviction that I realized, with what felt like sudden clarity, that something had to change. Unable to rent anywhere else due to my now terrible credit, and certainly not swimming in cash, I needed to secure a steady pay flow, stat. The band thing was a lot of fun, but getting paid forty dollars to play songs with my pants half-off didn't exactly qualify as "making it." However, I was aware that better-paying music-related gigs *did* exist and that they were *sort of* in the realm of what I wanted to be doing with my talents. That's right; I was ready to enter the exciting world of background piano gigging for weddings, cocktail hours, and bar mitzvahs. I knew that braving the obstacles posed by neurotic wedding planners, stressed-out parents, and the occasional keyboard malfunction would test my mettle, but the guaranteed payoff was significant: checks for two, sometimes three hundred dollars, and all the hors d'oeuvres I could want. Consume enough free hors d'oeuvres, some say, and you've scored yourself a free dinner.

From my experimental mixing of hip-hop with jazz in high school, I'd learned that the surest way to get people excited is to start them in a familiar place and then whisk them away. In action, this can be as simple as trying out various styles of music on your listeners and paying close attention to their reactions. For me, the first step was to figure out what people *wanted* to hear at a given event. I already knew lots of jazz standards, and through trial and error, I began to sift out the ones that non-musicians liked best. "My Romance," "Moon River," and "The Way You Look Tonight," for example, all proved popular in the greater Hartford cocktail hour scene. When people requested songs that I wasn't familiar with, I made sure to take note so that I could practice and prepare them for next time. I always did my best to match the vibe of the room; more subdued crowds received the classic ballad and love song treatment, while energetic crowds were served upbeat jazz and the occasional Billy Joel or Beatles tune.

The next step for me was to get leads—to locate the demographic that would want this type of entertainment. Some digging on Craigslist led me to discover its events section, which contains ads placed by individual photographers, event planners, and the like. Essentially, the section functions as a one-stop shop for anyone throwing a wedding or large party; surprisingly, this gold mine of client leads appeared to be largely untapped by musicians. Right away I built a webpage featuring a photo of me wearing a suit and a friendly expression and a solo piano audio file of "My Funny Valentine." I began drafting posts targeted at couples about to get married, with the goal of convincing them that hiring a pianist like me—presumably a class act with excellent credit who could play any song requested, from Gershwin to Billy Joel—would elevate their cocktail hour from conventional to something straight out of a celebrity wedding from Hollywood's glamorous Golden Age.

After a few trial posts and a handful of tweaks, the ad started garnering real results. Never one to shy away from an opportunity to break the rules, I developed a routine of refreshing the ad every other day so that it would sit near the top of the page, where it was more likely to be seen.

Before long, I was earning referrals from many of the individuals and event planners who'd hired me through the site. This happened thanks to three factors, and I can't emphasize enough how firmly I believe these should be standard operating procedure for *anyone* building a reputation in a creative field:

1. I showed up to the gig on time and appropriately dressed.
2. I was nice to the people who hired me.

3. I had my own keyboard, amplifier, and transportation. (I didn't own a car, but my fellow credit-delinquent friend Hobbes let me borrow his Dodge Neon.)

To this day, it saddens me when I encounter musicians who don't understand how crucial these three basic tenets are to finding employment. Throughout my life, I've met a lot of really fantastic musicians who unintentionally limited the amount of work they received by ignoring these basic rules. After a certain level of competence, above-and-beyond ability becomes superfluous on most commercial gigs. From the point of view of the person doing the hiring, it's far better to contract with a competent player who has a great, professional attitude than with a brilliant but irresponsible and egotistical musician who will likely require reining in and micromanaging.

No matter who you are or what you've accomplished, if you're working for someone else, you must always have humility about your role. Try looking at it like this: When you're hired to play background music, you're essentially filling the same role as an ice sculpture. Sure, you're playing music, but you're meant to blend in as atmosphere. No one throws a party and thinks, "Man, I'd really like to bring in an ice sculpture that shows up late and half-sculpted, refuses to pose in place and keeps sliding around, and then demands to be compensated in full despite pulling a premature meltdown and leaving before the night's over." Similarly, no one throws a party and hopes that the hired musical performer arrives without a suit, refuses to turn down the volume after being asked twice, and then insists at the last second on being paid in cash instead of by check because rent is due. If you agree to be an ice sculpture, be the best damn ice sculpture you can be.

I eventually acquired enough event work to pay my bills like the real adult that I was (at least in age), and you know what? I enjoyed the work much more than I had expected to. Of course, in addition to earning money, anyone who self-identifies as an artist also needs to be able to find inspiration in at least *some* aspect of what they do in order to be happy and succeed long term; creativity and talent will stagnate if neglected. I didn't see myself finding that kind of inspiration in the corner of a banquet hall, watching the mother of the bride yell at yet another event planner over a tablecloth. So, when I wasn't shooting covert, sympathetic glances at the latest victim without missing a beat in playing the music I'd been hired to provide, I kept an eye out for other, potentially more rewarding opportunities in my free time—which I found I had a lot more of now that I was no longer using it to creatively dodge calls from creditors.

Soon enough I found one that piqued my interest: a gig playing Sunday morning services at a Salvation Army–sponsored rehab center. It was in downtown Hartford, a rough-and-tumble part of town that most people I knew avoided. On the upside, it would be a steady and reliable gig, and I liked the idea of using my musical skills for good. I was a bit apprehensive my first day on the job, since I didn't know much in the way of Gospel music and had never met anyone who suffered from a serious drug addiction, but I donned my best suit, showed up on time, put a smile on my face (recall the first and second tenets above), and embraced the uncertainty... and how glad I am that I did. I was greeted by the choir director, a friendly, upbeat woman in her fifties whose obvious love for what she did worked wonders in putting me at ease. Together, we went over the center's binder of songs; there were a lot of them, and all but "Amazing Grace" were unfamiliar to me. Before I knew it, the parishioners had arrived, and it was time to begin. I hoped I wouldn't mess up too badly.

Coming from a small country town in New Jersey, where

crime was nonexistent save for the occasional cow tipping, I was nervous about performing at a rehab center, unsure whether the audience's troubled histories might make them less receptive to my eagerness to connect with them musically. Nothing could have been further from the truth: They were incredibly welcoming, and their response to my playing was *electric*. I played boogie-woogie piano solos in the middle of Gospel standards, and the entire room would get up on their feet and cheer and clap and dance along. The whole experience—everything about it—was completely the opposite of the background music gigs I was usually hired to do. The members of the parish called me "Brother Scott" and told me that they prayed for me to find recognition and success.

One week, after I mentioned offhand to a parishioner that someone had smashed the window of my leased Subaru Forester and stolen my keyboard, they held a moment of silence during the service to pray that I would be able to recover it. I was touched, but I also felt embarrassed; these people had *real* problems to worry about, and yet here they were, praying for *me*. It gave me a powerful sense of perspective on what it means to struggle.

I wound up playing the Salvation Army gig every week for the next year, and it always felt good: humbling, eye-opening, and gratifying. The folks there were the best audience I ever had. Knowing that my music was bringing them real happiness and hope inspired me to play more creatively and with more passion. It reaffirmed for me that I was meant to do *something* in music, something with the power to inspire and uplift, something that could—even if only temporarily—transcend the differences between people and bring us all together for one beautifully joyful moment. I was finally, truly ready to give music everything I had.

In the summer of 2006, I packed up my things and said a

bittersweet good-bye to my friends from all the various gigs I'd played over the years. Everyone at the Salvation Army center was ecstatic for me. Amid hugs and farewells, they told me that they were certain this next step would lead me to stardom.

I was to make a brand-new start of it in New York City.

And so I set off in my Subaru Forester, full of my earthly possessions and topped by a mattress tied to its roof, to the city that had lingered in the back of my mind ever since I'd visited it for the first time as a teenager. A few hours later, just as the sun was setting against a skyscraper-filled sky, the familiar cityscape came into view. It looked like a future of fantastic opportunities was sprawled out before me.

DEALING WITH FAILURE

We don't want the same things," my girlfriend of two years sobbed, gesturing around at the messy, cockroach-infested apartment that we shared. "Nothing has changed! You're never going to change!"

"I just need a little more time," I protested, though what I really felt was resigned.

Because she was right. We had begun dating at the end of college, and she had moved to New York with me in the hopes that I would mature into something resembling marriage material. Instead, in the year since we'd moved to New York City, I'd managed to run up a hundred thousand dollars in student loan debt, drop out of grad school, and fail to make a single meaningful contact that might further my career. Worse, I was having more and more trouble booking gigs. What had worked in Hartford—self-promotion and sourcing clients through Craigslist—wasn't cutting it in the much more saturated market of New York City, and so I resorted to indiscriminately mass-sending business cards and CDs (that likely went unheard) to every restaurant and banquet hall in town. The popular talent booking agencies weren't of much help, either; when I sent out a recording of myself playing a ragtime version of "Stairway to Heaven," I was met with a spate of flat-out rejections—including one blunt "nobody wants to hear that stuff." At one particularly desperate juncture, I even took to commuting back up to Hartford on a weekly basis, just so that I could take comfort in playing for familiar faces at familiar venues. It had become abundantly clear to me that making ends meet in New York City as a working jazz pianist was going to be far more difficult than I'd ever imagined. As an outsider in a city that attracted top talent from music schools all over the world, and where connections often carried more weight, even, than raw talent, no one was willing to open their doors for me.

"I'm really worried for you. You're twenty-six years old. How are you going to take care of yourself if you refuse to get a job?"

My girlfriend stood at the door with her pink suitcase, looking at me imploringly, but also with real pity. I didn't have a good answer for her because this was never part of the plan. I was supposed to come to New York and dazzle the city with my creativity before getting signed by a record label that would help spread my music around the world and send me on tour to prestigious jazz clubs.

"Good-bye," she said, closing the door.

Suddenly, it was just me, alone in an apartment that I couldn't afford, in a city that didn't care to know my name.

That night, the same empty feeling washed over me that I'd felt sitting on the curb outside my high school, waiting for my dad to pick me up after a night of watching my classmates dance from the sidelines.

... *What the hell am I doing here? I don't belong here* ...

Radiohead's "Creep" had never felt more apt.

Life generally doesn't go according to plan. This is a tough pill to swallow because a big part of being human is making plans and trying to anticipate, if not outright influence, the future. In my case, I had designed what I thought to be a *great* plan to gain a foothold in the New York City music scene. I'd applied and been accepted to a prestigious grad school with a great reputation for the arts, and I was certain that the program's high-profile faculty would immediately identify and help foster my talent while providing me with ample professional guidance and career opportunities.

Not so. The program, as it turned out, was in the midst of a chaotic time; the department head had stepped down, and the interim head hadn't yet proved capable of restoring any sense of order to the place. I had some good professors, but a number of my teachers canceled class regularly and seemed to fail to offer much in the way of career guidance to me and other students. I dropped out after a year and never went back; I'd made a painful, naive mistake in putting all my trust in a name rather than fully thinking through what I needed, which realistically was just another laboratory in which to carry out my musical experiments alongside other young, talented performers. No musician needs a degree testifying to his or her ability to play. *Every* musician, however, needs the networking and support system that comes from collaborating with ambitious, creative people on a daily basis.

And that's how I found myself in massive debt, with zero career prospects on the horizon, and with no girlfriend by my side now, either. My life was in shambles, but somehow I still more or less managed to look on the bright side. After all, I had my musical instruments, some recording equipment, and my own place to live: a basement apartment, in a building in Queens, owned by an older Greek woman named Agatha.

"I charge fourteen hundred dollars for the basement," she'd said when we first met. "But for you? Nine hundred. You look like a good boy, so I take care of you. But, let me tell you something— NO DRUGS!! You hear?"

Agatha was quite the character, and I mean that in the best possible way. Her entire family lived in the building, and under her guidance maintenance and repairs on the premises were generally carried out by these family members with varying degrees of competency. She had a strong maternal streak and would often leave food out for me...albeit in slightly inconvenient locations and often without any sort of heads-up. It was not unusual for me to return home after a weekend of gigging back in Hartford to find a leg of chicken propped on the air conditioner outside, or to find a bag of soggy bread tied to my car door on a rainy day, or to be greeted upon entry into my abode by a garbage bag stuffed with literally hundreds of discarded bagels from the shop she owned. The impromptu food bonanzas were an endless source of humor for me, and I eagerly awaited the next bestowal so that I could recount the story of it for friends and family. At the same time, though, Agatha's offerings, odd as they were, made me feel good. It was comforting to know that, in her own way, she was looking out for me and truly cared about my well-being. The city can be very isolating, and for me, especially, in the wake of so much disappointment, it had become exceedingly lonely. To have tried so hard at something only to flounder spectacularly had taken a serious toll on my psyche, and I was grateful to have some semblance—any semblance—of family around. And Agatha, from the instant she had me drive her to the bank to deposit my first rent check while she further admonished me to "be a nice boy" and "say no to the drugs," was definitely family.

My apartment was cold and unfinished, with essentially no natural light to speak of. It had few of the standard comforts of a typical apartment; there was no stove, and I slept on a mattress on the floor next to the boiler room, which doubled as a heat source in the winter months. And yet, despite all that it lacked, it had everything I needed. All I wished for was a room large enough to fit a drum kit, multiple keyboards, a PA system, my recording gear, and "A Great Day in Harlem," which I brought from New Jersey and hung on my wall as a visual reminder to stay inspired. Most of the neighbors didn't mind the noise of my practicing; the only real issue I had resulted from a disgruntled tenant calling the housing commission to report that I was possibly occupying an illegal apartment in the basement of her building. Agatha, advanced in years but ever the quick thinker, saved the day by explaining to all parties that I was her nephew. Well, all parties, that is, except for me, which led to this exchange:

AGATHA: Scott! From now on, when you see me, you call me "Aunt Agatha." It's very important. I tell them your parents are dead and you must stay with me to go to school.

ME: I don't know, Agatha, that feels a little weird. You know, because my parents are alive, and I dropped out of school, and...well...you're not my aunt?

AGATHA: (firmly) No! Do as I say. You must call me "Aunt Agatha."

ME: (resigned) Yes, Ag—I mean, Aunt Agatha.

Before long, I was holding jam sessions in that apartment, and I hosted a few parties there, too, the most memorable being a '70s roller disco–themed affair that had guests skating on the hard basement floor. It may or may not surprise you that Agatha encouraged the music and partying; she loved having young people visit the building, and she often dropped off gifts for us, such as a five-gallon vat of split pea soup and leftover Greek Easter bread. As a thank-you, I would pass along information about the vacant units in her building to everyone who came through; you just never know who might be in the market for an apartment that includes the occasional free meal. I may have been broke, but I was having a blast.

FINDING A NEW
WAY FORWARD

Midway through 2008, I arrived at a crossroads. I finally had enough consistent work, teaching piano lessons and playing cocktail hours and restaurants, to make ends meet in my cold little basement apartment in Queens, but the life I was leading was still worlds away from the glamor of New York City. I was surviving paycheck to paycheck and now solidly in my late twenties—far past the age where the "struggling artist" trope has any allure. My musician friends were mostly in the same boat as I, and one by one, they began abandoning their creative projects for more stable employment. But whereas they often seemed enthused about their new opportunities and content to leave behind their dreams, I felt unable to give up on my pursuit of a music career, no matter how much it was causing me to suffer.

And artistically, I *was* suffering. I was stuck. I began having visions of a future in which I was in my forties and still living in a basement, hustling for the next hundred-dollar gig, all the while railing against the "establishment" and bitterly blaming the unsophisticated audiences that failed to see the artistry of my career's work. Scarily, it didn't feel so far-fetched.

"I read an article in the *New York Times* about how today's college graduates are taking a much longer time to find employment," my mom said to me over the phone one day, as I sat on the couch preparing yet another CD package to send out to yet another Manhattan restaurant. "I guess it's just more difficult these days." I could tell how hard she was trying to be upbeat, and still I could sense the sadness in her voice.

This was not at all the life that I had envisioned for myself back when I was spending eight hours a day practicing piano so that I could gain the chops to reignite the world's love for classic jazz. There was a part of me that wondered if my dreams, encouraged by my supportive parents and helped along by so many others over the years, had ever been anything more than fantasy. Perhaps, I reasoned unhappily, this is what life really amounts to for us music kids: You peak early, you grow up, you find a "real job," and you settle down and wonder what might have been. Was there an alternative? I wasn't sure.

As my disillusionment with the plight of the musician's life in New York City bloomed and spread, I found myself looking for an escape hatch, a career that could provide the sort of stability my friends now entering law school were also seeking. On a whim, I picked up a copy of Stephen Hawking's *A Brief History of Time* at a local bookstore, with the goal of broadening my horizons a bit. It seemed to do the trick; reading about the wonders of the universe provided temporary respite from the doldrums of my daily existence. I soon discovered that despite my high school track record of solid D's in science, I really enjoyed reading about the origin of the universe and the physical laws that governed it. I didn't understand many of the finer, more complex arguments in the book, but it allowed me to meditate on the abstract, big-picture concepts of reality instead of fixating on the immediate difficulties I was having. Indeed, my career troubles seemed to miraculously retreat when considered alongside the sheer vastness of the universe. I was hooked.

I started digging deeper, next reading about great physicists like Albert Einstein and Richard Feynman. Forget Gordon Hunter; Einstein and Feynman were true rock stars; brilliant, free minds who led unconventional lives while pursuing greater truths about the mysterious universe in which we live. Feynman even had some musical interests; in a move that undoubtedly must have confused his peers, he spent a year playing bongos in South America. For the first time in a while, I felt inspired, and it got me wondering if I could somehow contribute to a noble and respected field like science in my own creative way.

Contemplating a return to higher education, I set out to spend the next year teaching myself calculus, the mathematical underpinning of physics. During breaks at my piano gigs, I worked hard at deriving equations and tried my best to internalize fundamental concepts. Just as practicing piano had functioned, for me, as an escape from the horrors of adolescent life a decade and a half prior, so studying physics provided me with an escape from my failure to launch a career as a musician. In early 2009, I sent in my application to CUNY Hunter College and was accepted to begin studies that fall as an undergraduate. It was time to face the music, gain some practical skills, and get myself a "real job."

In a strange twist, the promise of this impending escape hatch actually freed me up artistically. You see, in all those years that I'd seen music as my future, I'd been terrified of releasing anything less than stellar, lest it harm the reputation I had built for myself in my mind. As a result, I never released anything, too paralyzed by worry to permit myself to engage with that fundamental building block of creativity: risk.

But with the assurance that I was soon to become an

upstanding scholar of science, my capricious musical experiments lost their burdensome weight. They no longer mattered. And so it was that in May 2009 I set up a cheap Flip camcorder on a tripod and angled it down toward my bright red keyboard. Recently I had noticed many musicians gravitating to a video-sharing site called YouTube, which I had previously steered clear of because I had always believed myself to be too "professional" for a venue populated with so many amateurs. Since that was no longer an issue, I was curious to see how some of my more cutting-edge genre mixes would be received on there.

The piece I recorded that evening was a medley of ten '80s pop hits by ten different artists, including Madonna, Bon Jovi, and Dexys Midnight Runners. I had played ragtime medleys like this for my friends in the past, of course; it was my tried-and-true party trick. This particular iteration, though, I purposefully hadn't rehearsed. I may have shed my fear of failure, but I still retained pride in my composition ability, and I wanted to give myself the excuse of having improvised the whole thing on the fly in case I made too many mistakes. Besides, improvising was my preferred mode of playing anyway. I did have a rough idea of the transitions between songs in my head, and I had a list of the songs scribbled on some paper atop my Nord keyboard, for quick reference. Attempting to mimic the look of a saloon pianist, I dressed up in a waistcoat and tie for the occasion and, after a quick run-through, pressed the Record button, took my place at the keyboard, and stretched my fingers in an exaggerated fashion. I was off to the races.

I filmed a few takes before downloading the video to my laptop for reviewing. From the plastic-y creak of the keys picked up by the camera's onboard mic and its low-res rendering of me as an amorphous blob of uncombed hair, to the string of flubbed notes I'd made while attempting to play the medley at the upper limit of my speed, nothing about the video looked remotely professional. Still, I had nothing to lose. I uploaded it to YouTube under the username "ScottBradleeLovesYa," the first username to pop into my head, and hit Publish.

Nothing could have prepared me for what happened next.

HEY NOW, YOU'RE
A YOUTUBE STAR

June 3, 2009: It was a Wednesday that started like any other. I woke up to my alarm, threw on some clothes, and grabbed my backpack and one of the bagels from the giant bag Agatha had left for me before heading out into the world.

On Wednesday mornings, I ventured into Manhattan for my "day job," accompanying a singer-guitarist named Tim Kubart in music classes at a pre-preschool for some of Manhattan's most distinguished babies. It was exactly as you might imagine, should you ever find yourself imagining what a pre-preschool music class for elite infants looks like. We played songs at babies (not "for babies" because that would imply that they requested songs, and as advanced as their parents may have believed them to be, at the end of the day they were still...babies). As you also might imagine, they largely ignored us in favor of doing baby-like things, like crawling around the room and clumsily hitting each other with tiny, drool-coated fists. When they weren't ignoring us, the babies threw some pretty impressive tantrums, just like non-wealthy babies did.

It was a strange but amusing job, and Tim and I had fun with it. Together, we would improvise ridiculous, pop culture–themed lessons and perform them for our largely disinterested audience (but really, mostly, for our own entertainment). One morning, for example, we performed "The Itsy-Bitsy Spider" as if it were a duet between Eminem and Rihanna. Another time, in the much more advanced three-year-olds' music class, we paralleled the plot of MTV's *Jersey Shore* by pretending to work out and get a fresh haircut before finally letting loose at a dance party of fist-pumping proportions in "the club"—where "the club" amounted to Tim simply flicking the lights on and off while I played a medley of house music hits on the piano.

During the lunch break, I logged onto the staff computer to check my email for new comments on the YouTube video I had recently uploaded. I could hardly believe my eyes; unless there'd been some mistake, there were literally hundreds of emails notifying me of comments about it. I quickly loaded the video to see what was happening. It had gotten over twenty-five thousand views, and additional comments were appearing by the minute. Many of them referenced a certain "Neil Gaiman," whose name I promptly Googled. And that's when it all came together. Gaiman, the celebrated British author of *The Sandman*, *American Gods*, and *Coraline*, among other works, had, just a few hours earlier, while I was performing to an audience of infants, tweeted a link to my video with the caption "What the world needs now: Ragtime covers of Come on Eileen, etc."

If this was what overnight celebrity felt like, fifteen minutes wasn't going to be enough.

The rest of that workday was, basically, a lost cause (sorry, babies). I spent it obsessively refreshing my email for new comments while fielding calls from the handful of friends who had witnessed the video take off. I couldn't get out of pre-preschool fast enough that afternoon, and as soon as I got home, I glued myself to my computer to watch my small-time celebrity soar. I was now at thirty thousand views, and the comments were, for the most part, very positive, with "Amazing!" being the most commonly used adjective. One commenter mused on what life would be like if every song had a ragtime version. More than one viewer commented that she had spontaneously become pregnant as a result of watching my video. That seemed to be a bit of an extreme reaction to the sound of ragtime piano, but it was flattering nonetheless.

That night, I did what I do whenever something thrilling occurs in my life: I didn't sleep. Instead, I spent hours trying to process what had just happened and wondering if and how my life was going to change. For once in my life, I felt *relevant*. It was the same sensation I'd experienced back in eighth grade, when playing piano for my classmates earned me their respect and a round of boisterous cheers, except now it somehow felt more *real*—even if I couldn't see my audience.

The video went on to rack up sixty thousand views in total that week—a sum that was far greater than the total number of people who by that point in my career had *ever* seen me perform live. I briefly considered how I might profit from all the video traffic, but alas, I didn't have anything to sell, so instead I wrote a blog post about the video, in case anyone wanted to learn a bit about my background. In all honesty, I had no idea what any of this meant, or what to do with the attention, or even how much attention this really *was* when it came to the Internet. *Was I famous now?* I got my answer to that one real fast, when I mentioned my video to a couple on the subway I'd overheard talking about Neil Gaiman. "Cool," they said dully, before resuming their conversation.

So much for that.

This video, I soon realized, was just a starting point. I was a little disappointed that no one recognized me at the grocery store after my YouTube hit and that Agatha didn't look particularly impressed when I told her that I had made her building Internet famous. The video, it seemed, wasn't going to lead to immediate fame, wealth, or happiness. It did, however, inspire me to record a twenty-song version of the medley as my "iTunes debut." I wanted higher production quality this time, but I couldn't afford to rent a recording studio with a grand piano for a day. So, I lugged my mics and audio gear—that ever-present reminder of the credit card debt I'd accumulated in Hartford—to the music room at my old high school.

The resulting single, "Hello, My Ragtime '80s," netted me about a hundred fifty dollars in its first month on sale. No life-changing sum, but it was enough to give me hope that it *was* possible to record tracks, share them online, and have people willingly pay to consume them. This was passive income at its finest. For the very first time in my life, I had the ability to make money in my sleep. I liked that a lot.

Most importantly, the video allowed me to break free of a monster that had held me back for years—a monster that I never spoke of for fear that acknowledging it would render it even more omnipotent.

THE MONSTER CALLED
PERFECTIONISM

The most difficult battles we face in life are those we wage within. Self-doubt, feelings of unworthiness, and fear of rejection: This is the trifecta of demons that holds us back from reaching our full potential. We're not born with these demons; for proof of this, one need only look at how free and uncensored young kids are. By the time most of us reach adulthood, however, we've devolved into a tangle of insecurities and negative experiences.

From what I've seen and from what I've suffered, I'd wager that perfectionism hits artists the hardest. Artists—whose very calling is based on the expression of feeling—tend to be more introspective than your average human being and spend much more time living internally. Releasing a creative project out into the world requires ceding a part of yourself to the world and exposing it to the slings and arrows of external criticism. So, it's only natural that the artist, aware of the vulnerability and invitation for judgment inherent in the act of creating publicly, would take painstaking care to ensure that whatever is released into the world is as close as possible to "perfect." If left unchecked, this tendency to obsess and strive for perfection can lead the artist to devote months, if not years, to producing a single flawless creation. The truth of the matter, though, is that our actual creations will *never* be so perfect as we've dreamt them to be; they can only be perfected in the sense that, when released, they *exist*.

Sometimes, it takes *losing* control to *gain* control over this obsession with perfection. That my relatively unpolished ragtime medley went viral so quickly forced me to push past my aversion to making myself vulnerable to other people's opinions. Initially, the video received a tremendous amount of praise, but as it found its way to more sites and spread across the Internet, it began to garner a hefty dose of criticism, too. The mostly anonymous critics took aim at everything from my homegrown piano technique to my haphazard haircut (to be fair, both *were* fairly out of control in those days). It seemed bizarre to me that, given all the evils in the world, people would expend so much of their energy vocalizing anger at a stranger who was simply trying to provide them with a few minutes of entertainment, but at least I now had a solid hunch as to why signs reading "Don't Shoot the Piano Player" were deemed necessary in saloons. If you put yourself on the Internet, be prepared for strangers to fire shots:

"Horrendous, eh?"

"Nice setup, but you should really invest in a metronome…"

"Sloppy as hell."

And, my personal favorite: "You're amazing on that piano. Too bad you look like such a douchebag."

It was uncomfortable at first, reading these cutting remarks, and my initial thought was that I wanted to reply to the critics to defend myself. Thankfully, I was wise enough to understand that engaging in a shouting match with my critics and haters would not a good look make. Surprisingly, much to my relief, the sting of the criticism subsided after a few minutes. Whether that's because I'd grown a tougher skin lightning fast or found inner enlightenment and peace, I don't know. One thing I can tell you for certain: Empathy works wonders when dealing with the most brutal kind of criticism. The harshest of the negative feedback I received oozed with the kind of insecurity that had, for a long while, been lodged so deep within *me* that it had prevented me from sharing my music. I was able to recognize the ugly emotion and the place of fear that it was born from because once upon a time, I, too, had been at its mercy. The only difference was that I'd resisted the impulse to go on the Internet anonymously and be a jerk about it by taking it out on other people. The choice is always there.

In the end, it was the comments that made valid points about my shortcomings as a pianist that were a bit tougher to hear, but even those didn't seem to affect me much—at least not in the way they would have even a couple years earlier. The video, I came to see, was akin to a snapshot in time, and my performance in it was honest and genuine. By that measure, it was already perfect for what it was. I had no reason to defend it.

I came away from the whole experience with the perspective-shifting realization that I'd spent a good seven years—precious time that could have been used to create—in perfectionist limbo, rationalizing to myself that I just wasn't *ready*. Experiencing the criticism that I'd been shielding myself against for so long showed me how little it actually mattered. I vowed to continue to think of each new video as another snapshot in time, nothing more, and I'm proud to say I've kept that promise to myself.

If there's one lesson you take away from this story of my unexpected YouTube stardom, I hope it's this: You will never feel "ready" or "comfortable with" putting your work out there. It is so important to make peace with and internalize this idea. If you're a musician and you've just written a song that you're on the fence about, the best time to record it is right now. If you're a filmmaker and you want to make a movie but don't have the best equipment, the best time to begin making it is right now, with whatever equipment you can get your hands on. If you're reading this and have a feeling that this might apply to you, set my book aside, get up, and go do whatever creative project you've been putting off—you guessed it—right now.

Despite my glimpse of twenty-first-century Internet fame—a harbinger, I hoped, of more good things to come—I still struggled to create consistently and courageously at that point in my life. I was tired of feeling like fear had power over me, though, and so I made a rule for myself: Whenever I was having trouble working up the gumption to create something, I simply set a deadline for its completion and told my newfound fans about it, so that they'd help hold me accountable and follow through with it. I continue to put the rule into action to this day, and I urge you to do the same if ever you're feeling stuck. It's not unusual for me to announce the release of an album days or sometimes weeks before it's ready to go. Declaring deadlines helps me stay the course because to delay or cancel a release would mean disappointing my fans. The perfectionist monster in me still rears its head every so often, but my desire to never disappoint those who've put their trust in me is a much more powerful motivator.

My follow-up videos didn't create as much of a stir as that first medley did, but they were pivotal in my establishment of a new working format. I found that having concise, memorable titles was absolutely crucial; I needed to be able to describe each video in a way that would compel my prospective viewer to think, "Yeah, I'd be interested in seeing that." I learned that the medleys and nostalgia-inducing content were being shared like crazy, and so with the goal of creating even more of them, I teamed up with my saxophone-playing friend from college, Ben Golder-Novick. He was a brilliant improviser with a quick ear who, like me, appreciated a bit of silliness in his music; back in school, we were known for mashing up jazz standards with '80s riffs, Dave Matthews songs, and Wu-Tang Clan instrumentals. I'd gotten it into my head to do a "Nintendo Jazz Odyssey" video, and inviting Ben to collaborate with me on it felt like a no-brainer. Together, we developed and recorded jazz versions of popular Nintendo game soundtracks and synced them to video game footage. When the finished product went viral, I felt like I'd struck gold—if "striking gold" means getting a small blurb in *Nintendo Power* magazine, a feat that no doubt would have filled nine-year-old me with limitless awe and reverence. I breathed easy, knowing that with the success of this second video, I was safely out of "one-hit wonder" territory.

EMBRACING CHANGING
TECHNOLOGY

The social media landscape was rapidly changing just as I was beginning to find my footing in it. New sites and blogs dedicated to content curation were appearing daily, and social media platforms like Twitter and Facebook were gradually becoming more influential than traditional media. It was disorienting but exciting, and I saw in the chaos a real opportunity to make a name for myself as a musician for the social media age. In an uncharacteristic burst of organization, I made a spreadsheet of press contacts for all the media outlets that had shared my videos: *College Humor, Today's Big Thing, Digg, Reddit, BuzzFeed, 22 Words, The Daily What, The Awesomer, Huffington Post*... the list went on. Every time I went live with a new video, I would blast a link and a short note to all these outlets, hoping that even just one of them would run with it. In the process, I noticed that when one of the bigger websites ran a feature on something, all the smaller outlets would soon follow suit. Determined to make the most of this trickle-down effect, I put myself in the shoes of the editors and did my part to craft attention-grabbing headlines for them that could be quickly cut and pasted, in case they chose to write me up. The strategy seemed to work pretty well;

and while I never actually met any of the editors who shared my videos, I felt like we developed a solid, chummy rapport by email, despite my blatant self-promotion.

These videos of mine that they so graciously helped to hype ranged from a sepia-toned *Jersey Shore* trailer (I realize this is the second time I've referenced *Jersey Shore*; rest assured, it will not be the last) that played over a ragtime treatment of an EDM song; to a beatbox flute and electric piano mashup of Notorious B.I.G.'s "Big Poppa" with the *Harry Potter* theme; to a five-minute sax-and-piano medley of the *Pulp Fiction* soundtrack. The only commonality among all three was their vaguely jazz- and pop culture–oriented vibe. I was primarily preoccupied with pushing the creative envelope to see just what was needed to gain traction and go viral. To learn what worked, I did what a lot of business people refer to as "A/B testing," although I had never learned that term, so at the time I didn't know there was an official, alphabet-inspired name for what I was doing. As far as I was concerned, I was just going through the same meticulous motions I'd once undertaken to figure out jazz piano: trying a bunch of different combinations of ideas, seeing which combinations got me closer to my desired goal, and continuing to innovate from there. I experimented with video length (three minutes or under seemed to be the sweet spot for most attention spans), titles (jamming in oft-searched terms helped to get views but only when the content was actually related to those terms), and lighting (uploading certain videos in black and white or stylizing them in old-timey filters helped dress up the videos but only as a once-in-a-while thing). None of my methods were too scientific or precise; really, I just paid attention to the feedback I received— the non-insulting, constructive feedback, that is—and responded accordingly.

I hadn't quite put *all* of my music career eggs in the YouTube basket...yet...but at the same time, I was meeting with enough success on the platform that I didn't even think twice before dropping the idea of starting school for physics that fall. Something exciting was brewing—I could feel it. I was playing a great deal more piano gigs on the regular, and I was starting to make a bit of money on them by leveraging my online following to book higher-paying venues. My favorite gig was a weekly slot I secured for myself at Robert Restaurant in Columbus Circle, where I was paid handsomely (in money and in free food) to perform three hours of whatever solo piano pieces I wanted. It was a life I could get used to, and I wasn't the only one who was pleased with the way things were going.

"This is the most lovely place! I always dreamed you would play in a place like this," my mom exclaimed after my dad took her to New York City to hear me perform at the restaurant. She was beaming with pride.

The restaurant became yet another laboratory for me, and I used it to explore the concept of musical *mashups*: combinations of different songs that share similar themes. I developed a go-to format for my weekly sets at Robert, sticking to pure jazz in the first hour; a mixture of jazz peppered with a bit of classic rock in the second; and in the third and final hour, a no-holds-barred mashup assault on the senses that ventured into the edgier terrains of gangsta rap, '90s television themes, and beyond. The restaurant staff played a sizable role in my set planning, often slipping me hand-jotted notes filled with ideas. "Mashup Aerosmith and Music Theatre," one requested. " 'Girls Just Wanna Have Fun,' but sad," another read.

That the restaurant was located on the top floor of the Museum of Arts and Design meant that celebrities passed through frequently, and whenever they did, I would try to incorporate them into the show—usually without their consent. When Alan Alda came in to dine one evening, he did so to the tune of the theme from M*A*S*H* played in fourteen different styles. At the end of the night, he graciously tipped me a twenty, and I responded by playing the theme once again as he made his way to the elevator, as exit music.

Fresh off my first string of YouTube successes, I was antsy to think up additional unique ways of harnessing technology to bring my passion for "vintage" music to new audiences. I learned about Ustream, a streaming video interface that was popular at the time, and began using it to broadcast my piano playing over the Internet. One night, feeling extra inspired to experiment with my set, I brought my laptop with me to the restaurant, placed it on the piano, and spent the last hour of the three taking song requests over the Ustream chat interface. I posted a link to the broadcast on my Facebook page, and before long I had hundreds of viewers writing to me with their requests—while the restaurant's patrons, unaware of the online concert I was conducting before their very eyes, continued to dine per usual. Well, for the most part, that is. I'll never forget the night when an elderly patron wandered over to the piano mid-broadcast and stared directly into the webcam at the top of my laptop screen.

"What's all this here?" he asked, quizzically, gesturing at my setup.

"HEY, OLD MAN," someone instantly wrote in the chat feed. The old man gave me a confused look. I shrugged my shoulders sheepishly and launched into the Neil Young hit by the same name.

If you had told me back in high school that when I turned thirty I would mostly be playing concerts for strangers on the Internet and making YouTube videos, I would probably have recoiled in horror at this vision of a career gone horribly awry (after asking what YouTube was, of course). However, in reality,

I was extremely fulfilled. I had stumbled upon a way to do something I had long dreamed of: turning my background music gigs into genuine concerts with an actual audience. The only difference was that the concert venue existed virtually; the real-life audience only offered occasional applause here and there, punctuated by the occasional confused stare into the webcam as they passed.

Besides the curious old man who'd sauntered over to investigate my setup that first night, no one else at Robert seemed bothered by the streaming sessions I'd taken to hosting—even when technical difficulties and dropped Wi-Fi signals occasionally delayed my start times. The staff knew that something exciting was happening, even if it was a little strange, and often involved ragtime renditions of Rick Astley's "Never Gonna Give You Up." I had set up a new laboratory in an unlikely location—at the piano in the corner of the restaurant—and was furiously attempting to redefine the term "cocktail pianist."

Once, while wrapping up a live session, a diner who'd been watching me all night with amazement strolled over and asked for my card. The next day, he texted me and introduced himself as Kai Tao, former hedge fund president-turned-entrepreneur. Without any further preamble, he invited me to demonstrate what I was doing with interactive music broadcasting at the upcoming TEDxOrangeCoast in Orange County, California. His proposal completely caught me off guard; I'd performed for other people's enjoyment too many times to count, but never before had I been presented with an opportunity like this—to speak about the inspiration and process behind my music as an innovative *artist*, not a cocktail pianist—and I wasn't sure I could handle it. I'd be damned, though, if I was going to forgo the chance to appear in front of thousands of influential people who could help my career. I accepted on the spot and got to work. I had a kernel of an idea, and I needed to make it a reality—fast. I would build my very own customized streaming site (which, in my head, I'd already named *Emote CTRL* because why not put the cart before the horse), so that I would have some kind of visual to present with my talk. I had no idea what this entailed, but I called a couple friends who did and gave them the timeline for this project. In just a couple months, I'd be boarding a flight to California to give my very first speaking gig as an innovator, despite having no real credits to my name. But imposter syndrome be damned—it was starting to feel like I might be going places.

Touching down in sunny Los Angeles was something of a culture shock. Everyone seemed to simultaneously exude both success and laid-back relaxation. The people were also *a lot* friendlier than the brusque New Yorkers I'd grown used to. Kai—an enthusiastic natural connector—took me under his wing and brought me around to meet his friends in the entertainment business. At a dinner party the evening before the talk, I was introduced to an entrepreneur named Evan Lowenstein. In what felt like a serendipitous encounter, I learned that he was the founder of the online concert venue StageIt, which had, in large part, inspired the design of the website I'd built for the talk. Evan told me about how he'd gotten his project off the ground and about his previous life as a pop star. He had a twin brother, Jaron, who'd just made the switch from performing to management and was looking to sign up-and-coming talent. Together, as Evan and Jaron, they'd had a massive Billboard hit in 2001: "Crazy for This Girl." This he revealed to me with zero pretension and total casualness.

LA was proving itself to be every bit as surreal as I'd envisioned it would be.

I was beyond nervous about delivering my talk. I hadn't exactly accomplished anything of note in my career, and I'd never done any public speaking. The longer I fixated on these two truths, the

 63

more apprehensive I became. Luckily, the event organizers had thought to set me up with an acting coach, who would help me edit and fine-tune the timing of my speech. But between trying to memorize my lines verbatim and practice delivering them with the almost unnatural level of enthusiasm my coach was insisting on, the rehearsal left me feeling even *less* comfortable when my turn came to hit the stage.

I cringe when I watch that talk today—particularly at my halfhearted attempt to jokingly shush the audience—but all in all, it went fairly well, especially given my lack of experience and fraying nerves. In typical, cutting-it-close tech industry fashion, *Emote CTRL* was finished mere hours before the conference commenced. It worked as planned, though, and I even received a partial standing ovation after closing out my demonstration with a mashup of "Bohemian Rhapsody" and "What a Wonderful World." After succeeding in not crashing and burning onstage *and* in making what felt like a solid impression on the very important people of the business world who were in attendance, I was able to walk away with a new sense of purpose and a more secure sense of self. I was going to take these silly online experiments and turn them into a profitable *business*.

Returning to NYC with an entrepreneurial charge zipping through me and my inhibiting perfectionism finally in check, I decided the time had come to release my first solo piano album, *Mashups by Candlelight*. As you probably could guess, I used Robert Restaurant as my studio, bringing a flash recorder and two condenser mics to the recording session—which was actually just another night at the restaurant. The tracks I recorded offered a thoughtful and striking contrast to my earlier, more frenetic ragtime transformations. I'm inclined to call my playing more "mature," but to describe a mashup of the viral "Trololo" song and a popular tune from *Sesame Street* as "mature" might qualify as a stretch.

Mature or not, I took pleasure in coming up with clever names for the album's mashups; a Rihanna/Radiohead combo became "We Found Love in a Creepy Place," and a Coldplay/Tears for Fears mashup became "When I Ruled the Mad World." The finished product of my Robert recording session was a complete solo piano album that captured my sensibilities as a pianist pretty nicely. I released the album to my fans online, and by the end of the day, I'd made over two hundred dollars in sales, which was about the same sum that I would have earned playing a three-hour gig on the piano. When I woke the next morning and checked my email, I was delighted to see that I'd sold another forty dollars' worth of downloads overnight—concrete evidence that I was, indeed, making money in my sleep. Now *that* was an exciting development.

Looking back, I can see now that those early days on You-Tube were my artistic equivalent of "naked baby photos." Many artists hate their naked baby photos, often doing everything in their power to ensure that their early work is never discovered in order to create the illusion that they sprung forth into this world fully formed, like Athena from the head of Zeus. ("Mythology 101" was one of the few classes in high school I never cut.) I think this inclination artists have to bury what's rough and not yet fully formed is a huge mistake. Fans *want* to witness the growth and maturation of the artists they love; they *want* to see the messy false starts, and they recognize that these early works are intended to be representative not of an artist's entire output but a piece of it. And that piece—every piece—is essential to understanding and appreciating the whole. A body of work, no matter how masterful, is nothing without its individual parts.

FROM PIANIST
TO PRODUCER

Even with a few viral videos and a TEDx talk to my name, I still thought of myself as a pianist—and only a pianist. After all, it was my piano playing that was getting me attention on the Internet. It's a strange phenomenon, but meeting with even a minor degree of success and validation in one field (or, in this case, on one instrument) can make it harder to venture away from that comfort zone and into uncharted territory than if no amount of success or validation had been experienced at all. It took a prominent figure in the video game industry pointing out to me my skill as an arranger before I was able to embrace it in myself, along with the enticement of a top-secret project requiring that I put that skill to use, for me to shrug off my identity as "only a pianist" and step into something less restrictive.

Internet trends have a history of being fleeting, and so I feared my popularity on the web would fade, someday, as quickly as it had arrived. At the same time, though, I was hopeful that someone in the entertainment world would take note of what I was doing with my mashups and offer me a job. And then, in April 2010, my wish was granted.

A man named Jim Bonney, who was the audio lead for a

company called Irrational Games, had reached out to me by email after seeing my '80s-hits-as-ragtime compilation video. He wondered whether I might be interested in putting my skill of turning modern songs into ragtime to work on a big project that he was developing. I wasn't familiar with many video games post–*Super Mario Kart*, but a quick Google search confirmed that Irrational Games was a well-known video game studio. Intrigued, and feeling confident that this was a real lead, I set up a phone call with him to find out more.

Jim explained that the project would involve my demoing a bunch of songs from the '70s and '80s in a turn-of-the-century piano style, and if the game's legendary creative director, Ken Levine, felt that my material worked, it would end up in the game itself. Due to the secrecy and speculation that surrounds popular video game releases, I would have to sign a nondisclosure agreement and keep my participation in this project secret for the next couple years, until the game was released. I was told that I would be paid well for all of this, though the fee had yet to be determined.

When I got off the phone, I drew in a long, deep breath. This was the biggest professional opportunity I'd ever had, and I was determined to knock it out of the park. When it came to contracts, I was a complete neophyte, so the first thing I did was call a lawyer friend to get some advice. I had no idea how to negotiate a contract or even what deal points to include; the extent of my previous business negotiations had, for the most part, revolved around whether I could score a free meal after I'd finished playing a gig. I also contacted a few other arrangers who'd done music for film in the hopes that they'd let me pick their brains.

Over the years, I've made a habit of asking professionals with unlike areas of expertise for advice whenever I find myself venturing out of my comfort zone and into theirs for the first time. It's a habit that's served me well time and again—and certainly far better than letting ego stand between me and the information I need. There's no shame in allowing yourself to lean on others' expertise and become the student again; the only shame would be in not returning the favor should *your* wisdom be sought out someday. Most people—myself included!—love doling out wisdom, especially on subjects they've dealt with for most of their professional lives. It's a big, confusing world out there, especially in the entertainment industry, and it's important to actively develop for yourself a team of unofficial advisors that you can turn to for help in navigating the myriad decisions and dilemmas you'll undoubtedly encounter in life.

As I said, handling serious contracts was far, far outside my wheelhouse, and so it was an exciting milestone for me when I negotiated my first work-for-hire agreement as an arranger. The fee was much larger than any I'd received before, for any type of project. For fun, I included in my notes to the contract a request that my likeness be featured as an in-game character. They made no promises on that one, but they also didn't say "no."

I didn't know so much as the name of the game or even its general plot; Jim just selected a handful of songs from the '70s and '80s and told me to go to town on them. I set up my apartment as a makeshift studio, connecting my keyboard to my computer and recording simple demos of each song. I toed the line, intent on making the demos sound as authentically period as possible, even when it meant dialing back my own piano style. "Tainted Love," for instance, got a bluesy Jelly Roll Morton treatment, while I imagined "Shiny Happy People" with an Al Jolson–style Great Depression vibe, in the tradition of upbeat songs like "Happy Days Are Here Again."

Much to my relief, Jim loved the arrangements. He even found an incredible singer named Miche Braden to sing a Bessie Smith–style blues vocal on "Tainted Love," which we recorded in Studio B at Avatar Studios in New York City.

Whenever I think back on that experience at Avatar, I break out into a huge smile. It was a fantastic day and probably one of my favorite memories ever. I can see it now with perfect clarity: Miche in the vocal booth at Studio B, cheekily ad-libbing, "Oh, play that piano, Scotty Boy!!" to the piano track I'd recorded. Having grown up in Detroit during the Motown era, Miche truly embodied the stories of the songs she sang. She'd received music lessons from Earl Van Dyke of the Funk Brothers in her youth and had lent her voice to many soul records in the '70s and '80s, before becoming a star of the musical theatre stage in New York City. Her recent portrayal of Bessie Smith in *The Devil's Music* had earned her a Drama Desk nomination for "Best Actress in a Musical," and it was through a YouTube clip of this show that Jim learned of her powerful voice.

"I bet it's a treat to hear that voice singing over your piano," Jim said, observing my delight. He was beyond right. It was the first time I had ever recorded one of my "vintage" song arrangements with a vocalist, so automatically it was going to have special significance for me. But that this vocalist just happened to be a legend—well, it elevated the experience to utterly new heights. At points during the recording session, I had to silently remind myself that this was real life because it all just felt so beyond my wildest dreams. When Miche leaned into the high notes with the full power of her voice, I got intense chills. It was one thing to play these arrangements on piano, but it was something else entirely to hear them interpreted by an incredible singer.

In the end, many of my arrangements for *BioShock Infinite* (yes, Jim finally told me the game's name) wound up getting cut, mostly due to the difficulty of securing rights from the publishers of the original songs. This bummed me out a little, but the immense pride I felt for the tracks that *did* make it in stopped me from dwelling on the disappointment too long: "Tainted Love," "Shiny Happy People" (which, fittingly, featured an Al Jolson impersonator named Tony Babbino), the jazz standard "After You've Gone," and a waltz version of the Tears for Fears hit number "Everybody Wants to Rule the World." That last one I pictured being sung by an Irish tenor, and I recorded myself doing my best impression of just that as a temporary vocal on the demo. To my surprise, Ken Levine took such a liking to it that he wound up using it in the game. If you're playing and make it to the end, stick around for a few minutes; you'll hear me singing in my best old-timey voice as the closing credits roll.

In March 2013, after a few worrisome delays, *BioShock Infinite* was released—at long last—to critical acclaim. The anachronistic pop songs I'd worked so hard on were a big hit with players—and with the fictional characters who inhabited *BioShock*'s world, too. That's right: They'd been factored into the storyline as the purported compositions of a man named Albert Fink, who infamously stole hit songs from the future and passed them off as his own. Fink's reputation loomed large in Columbia—the fictional world that provided the setting for the game—despite making only one physical appearance in the game. It was never outright confirmed for me, but it would seem that my request for an in-game character had been honored: His eyes bear a striking resemblance to my own.

Working on *BioShock Infinite* was thrilling and gratifying for so many obvious reasons, but it was perhaps the quiet, personal revelation it led me to have that made me appreciate it the most: It helped me to understand that my YouTube experiments could be much more than clever, ephemeral viral videos. *BioShock* afforded me the ability to add renowned vocal talent to my arrangements, and by doing so I came to see—for the first time and with such clarity—that what I produced could stand on its own as great music, gimmicks aside. Suddenly, I no longer viewed myself as merely a pianist. I had become, in my own eyes, a producer.

FINDING INSPIRATION
IN THE MOST
UNLIKELY PLACES

want to thank you all…"

I was standing onstage in a foreign country, speaking to a thousand cheering fans who'd congregated that day to see us perform. People were dancing and holding aloft signs, adorned with the name of our group and lines of lyrics from some of the more crowd-pleasing songs we play. Behind me, my band was jamming on a Motown groove that sounded a bit like "Heat-wave" by Martha and the Vandellas. Only it wasn't "Heatwave"; it wasn't even one of our songs. In fact, it was "How You Remind Me" by the band Nickelback, and *my* band, A Motown Tribute to Nickelback, was playing at a major Canadian music festival.

Allow me to digress for a minute before explaining how I found myself in this amazing situation. As you may or may not know, Nickelback occupies that most notable position in the pantheon of modern music: the position of being at once extremely successful and extremely reviled. Have you ever witnessed an otherwise reasonable, level-headed person become downright enraged when the topic of Nickelback comes up? Well, I have, and let me tell you, it's highly amusing. While I perhaps never went out of my way to listen to their songs or see them play, I also couldn't get onboard the Nickelback Hate Wagon (and not just because it was at full capacity already).

In the scheme of things, Nickelback actually does the "band" thing very well—they play their instruments and sing with skill, they put on a great show for their fans, and, as far as I know, they don't go around kicking puppies. This might come as something of a disappointment (no, not the puppy part; what I'm about to say), but I have a soft spot for performers who get bashed by critics. The criticism leveled at mainstream acts has the reputation of being harsh and indiscriminate, with bands often judged not just on the basis of their musical ability but also for what they *represent*.

Watching an inoffensively mainstream act achieve such soaring heights of success has a way of throwing into stark relief the fact that many brilliant, boundary-pushing artists will never receive a fraction of such attention. Critics, meanwhile, seem to justify their vitriol as a tool by which to restore order in the world and knock obscenely successful performers down a peg. It's one thing to be of the mind that Nickelback is sort of bland; it's a whole other thing to condemn them as the "worst band in the world." I've been to quite a few open mics and dive bars in my day, and trust me when I say that Nickelback is *far* from the worst band in the world.

Regardless of my feelings about Nickelback, and regardless of whether you agree, you're no doubt still wondering how they came to factor so prominently in my life story that they've got their own chapter. Pull up a chair.

In the fall of 2011, tens of thousands of Detroit residents were so incensed by the news that Nickelback was booked to play their hometown Lions' Thanksgiving Day halftime show that they turned to that comfortably low-investment form of activism championed by Millennials everywhere: an Internet petition. Indeed, a change.org petition that cited Detroit's rich Motown history and demanded that a more suitable musical act take Nickelback's place *was* making the online media rounds. I sensed a massive opportunity to exploit this slightly ridiculous headline for viral video glory.

The brainstorming session that led to A Motown Tribute to Nickelback took place over lunchtime sandwiches in a SoHo grocery store. The musicians in attendance: Tim Kubart, my colleague from the pre-preschool music program, drummer friend Chip Thomas, and me.

I raised the topic of the Nickelback drama and proposed that we record a Motown version of the band's "How You Remind Me." My thinking was, it would be a great nudge to Nickelback and the hostile change.org petitioners to reconcile their differences—that, and it would likely result in a bounty of media coverage for us. Tim and Chip wholeheartedly agreed that this was a terrific idea, with Tim suggesting that I include a tambourine player on the track, since a lot of televised musical performances in the '60s included a square tambourine player enthusiastically bopping to the beat.

"I own a tambourine," Tim volunteered, after a beat.

"Perfect!" I said. "Now I just need a percussionist who can play it."

"I could play it," Tim said.

I winced. Tim was a very good guitarist and singer, but I had heard him attempt to play drums before. I didn't think that was something we needed to subject the entire state of Michigan to.

"Yeah...um...I'll let you know."

Setting aside my misgivings about Tim on tambourine, I focused on the bigger challenge: where to find a soul singer who could convincingly channel that Motown sound and really sell the arrangement I'd put together. Miche would have been perfect, but she was in Boston; it was the early days of my burgeoning career as a producer, and I wasn't yet confident enough in my abilities to bring a superstar vocalist over state lines—and to cover a Nickelback song, no less. With less than forty-eight hours until Thanksgiving and the clock ticking, I had nearly resigned myself to the sad fact that A Motown Tribute to Nickelback would exist only in my dreams.

Then I remembered Drue Davis.

A hip-hop producer, songwriter, and emcee, Drue was based in Brooklyn, and I'd had the pleasure of making his acquaintance a few months earlier on a slightly random project: a Yacht Rock tribute band in which we both performed. Yes, I got my first taste of Drue's exceptional voice when he was channeling Michael McDonald singing "What a Fool Believes." His voice was smooth and soulful, and he exuded a conviction and passion when performing that came from his roots singing in church. Above all, he was a guy with a big heart who loved making music with friends. I gave him a call.

"I don't know, man....I got my sister coming over for Thanksgiving dinner, and I have to do all the cooking. It has to be tomorrow?"

Figuring it'd be a tough sell because of the holiday, and not wanting him to feel awkwardly put on the spot, I made sure to bookend my invitation with a gentle, repeated plea that he "just think on it." To my surprise, he said he was game pretty much right away. Now I just needed to cobble together the rest of the band. I had enough mics to add drums, bass, and sax, but I had no sense of how staging an entire band in my living room would actually *sound*—besides loud. It was an ambitious scheme, and one that was certain not to please my embittered upstairs neighbors, who as you may recall were the ones respon-sible for my current identity as Agatha's newly orphaned nephew.

For bass, I recruited another musician I knew from college, Adam Kubota. Adam was a few years older than me; he'd been at Hartt for graduate work at the same time that I was entering as a freshman. We had traveled in different social circles but were uniquely, weirdly bonded by dating two sisters who also went to our school. Adam's girlfriend didn't like that her sister was dat-ing me, and my girlfriend didn't like that Adam was dating her sister. All of this dislike was very much out in the open, and it was something that Adam and I would occasionally joke about. (Looking back on it, they were totally justified in their feelings that neither of us was great boyfriend material.) Adam and I also bonded by doing private gigs together around town, including the hilariously stressful experience of playing a bar mitzvah in Hartford only to learn halfway through that we had been playing the wrong bar mitzvah at the wrong synagogue.

"Okay, so you need me to learn a Nickelback song to perform in your basement. This is where a master's degree in upright bass performance has taken me, huh?" he asked now, with character-istic snark.

Adam was a good sport about doing crazy gigs with me from time to time, but that's not to say he was ever thrilled to get my calls. Most of the shows that I'd talked him into playing in the past few years had been slightly ridiculous, largely unpaid, and often involved someone dressed, inexplicably, in costume—usually me as Thomas Jefferson or another friend as a giant koala.

Next, I brought in Allan Mednard, a talented young drummer I'd met on a jazz gig. Allan had been featured in my thirtieth birthday video—a one-take version of "Imagine" that I filmed on the street where I grew up—and he'd become my go-to drummer for gigs around town. To round out the ensemble, I called up my friend from that fateful first gig at Walmart, sax player Steve Ujfalussy.

With Adam on bass, Allan on drums, Steve on sax, and—with some reluctance on my part—Tim on tambourine, I had my band, and on the evening of November 23, we gathered in my basement abode to record.

I'd splurged not so long before on a new Canon EOS 60D DSLR camera as an upgrade from my cheap Flip camcorder, and I was excited to put it to the test. Recording went fairly smoothly but ended abruptly at 11 p.m., when the upstairs neighbor started pounding on my door and screaming at us to stop. We obliged and packed up, lest I create more trouble for Aunt Agatha, and I got to work editing.

The next morning was Thanksgiving, and I had an early gig at Robert Restaurant, which overlooked the Macy's Thanksgiving Day parade route. This was my second year of doing this; I treated it as a fun challenge wherein I would attempt to play the theme music of every float as it passed by. Some, like Snoopy and SpongeBob, were easy. Others, however, proved to be more of a challenge; Hello Kitty got the *Sailor Moon* theme song, and Buzz Lightyear got "Space Oddity." (By now, my perfectionist days were over.) After my shift, I raced back to Astoria to release the new video and then drove home to New Jersey to spend what was left of the holiday with my parents and sister.

I logged on to my parents' computer to check the view count as soon as I arrived, and a familiar feeling of excitement washed over me. The video had racked up twenty thousand views in a matter of hours, and it was already being featured in major—albeit Canadian—publications such as the *Vancouver Sun* and the *Calgary Herald*. The comments on the video ranged from the hilarious to the abusive, but a theme was quickly emerging across them: an enthusiastic endorsement of the inclusion of the hyperactive "Tambourine Guy."

Now, if you're watching the video after viewing many later appearances by Tambourine Guy, it's clear that this is as restrained a performance by Tim as it gets. But for newcomers to the character, it was just over the top enough to have viewers speculating on whether it was all an act or if this man was genuinely that enthused to be playing tambourine in this video. The beautiful thing is that both interpretations are correct. The sheer joy that Tim radiates during his performances as Tambourine Guy is infectious. There've been times when he's made an appearance at a show, and I've felt as surprised and excited as the audience when he walked onstage, even when I knew he was going to be there.

At first glance, it's ridiculous to see Tim paired with so many phenomenal singers and musicians, but after seeing him in action, it actually makes perfect sense. Tim embodies the ethos of Tambourine Guy like a champ, representing the desire of every audience member to be onstage, performing alongside so many great musicians—regardless of who they are. Tambourine Guy is living the dream, and you can't help but root for him for it. He also represents what A Motown Tribute to Nickelback came to symbolize in my musical development: the commitment to always have fun in whatever I create. After all, having fun is contagious.

A Motown Tribute to Nickelback was a huge success, landing me all over the Internet as the "Motown Nickelback Guy." I even gave a pseudo-satirical, academia-like interview about it to the *Village Voice*, tapping into some variation of the Gordon Hunter character from my college days. The biggest surprise to come of the whole nutty idea, however, was a phone call from a woman named Lara, a booking agent for Live Nation, North America's biggest concert promoter.

"We're booking a festival in British Columbia called 'Live at Squamish,' and we wanted to see if A Motown Tribute to Nickelback could perform," she explained, audibly attempting to suppress a chuckle, lest I take my life's work of revamping Nickelback too seriously.

"I would love to...but, just so we're clear, we're not actually a band. We only do that one song."

"Don't worry, I know. I've been following the story. Do you think you could do other Nickelback songs, too, though, if you had the time?"

"Sure," I said, as another idea dawned on me, and I began to gush. "So, I also do jazz versions of contemporary pop songs. I bet I could make a bigger show out of this. And I've got this video game thing, it's a secret, but—"

"Actually," she said, cutting my daydream short, "we're only looking for Nickelback songs."

Foiled, I had been pigeonholed yet again. First, I was Ragtime '80s Piano Guy, and now I was Motown Nickelback Guy. I felt for the "Where's the Beef?" lady.

Despite my initial misgivings, it *was* a neat opportunity. After a few emails and phone calls, A Motown Tribute to Nickelback was officially booked for Live at Squamish, a legitimate festival headlining real acts, like Chromeo and The Tragically Hip.

Since we had no press photo or bio, and Live Nation was hesitant to use the low-resolution video still that I'd provided, I organized an impromptu, faux-dramatic photo shoot for us in The Cloisters. Tim was the only one smiling, of course. I also drafted a bio describing us as a group that "painstakingly translates every song in the Nickelback catalogue into the Motown genre." I liked to think of us as some kind of bizarre fraternal order of mad scientists, dissecting every new Nickelback song and turning out Motown remakes.

Lara and Live Nation helped us assemble all the press materials we needed to qualify as a legitimate act, but that didn't mean everyone viewed us that way. When our name appeared on the festival fliers, most people assumed it to be a joke played by a disgruntled intern and had a good laugh about it in the comments section of the festival's Facebook page. The solution, I decided, was for us to record an album; after all, we needed to learn a set's worth of Nickelback songs regardless, and anything we could get online before then would help to build our fan base. But making a full album required first having the money to do it. My savings were still paltry, and the festival fee didn't even cover our flights to Vancouver, so I turned to Kickstarter to raise the funds.

I'm not sure whether the hundreds of people who pledged to the Motown Tribute to Nickelback Kickstarter were genuine fans or just supporters of weird projects in general, but either way, we easily cleared our goal of raising a few thousand dollars. We were ecstatic, but there wasn't much time to bask in the glory of our Kickstarter success; we had a big show to work toward and an album to plan.

So began the Summer of Nickelback.

When it comes to remaking modern songs in older styles, especially modern songs that have a less-than-sterling reputation in the public's eye, there's a fine line to be trod between tribute and parody. Though I recognized and appreciated the humorous aspects of the Motown Nickelback concept, I never wanted the project to drift too far toward parody. I was lucky to have bandmates who felt the same way. A true professional, Drue was able to set aside ego and shake off his friends' ribbing when he took on the not-insignificant task of memorizing the lyrics to eight Nickelback songs. I've learned that there's something much more admirable about taking these song transformations seriously and not giving in to peer pressure to deliver everything with a wink and a nod. That it's possible to celebrate and explore much-maligned songs without mockery has become something of a guiding principle for me whenever I'm approaching new material.

In addition to recording the album in Brooklyn, we also shot a few episodes of a mockumentary titled *The Road to Squamish*. We had fun playing exaggerated versions of ourselves and filming short sketches around Astoria. (The trope of the band that takes itself way too seriously has always appealed to me.) We wanted to make a great impression and put on an awesome show, but at the same time, I was still hesitant to take my own work *completely* seriously. In my mind, we were a troupe of musical pranksters, thumbing our noses at the establishment and willing to piss off both Nickelback fans and haters alike in our quest to make interesting music.

We departed from JFK two days before the festival began, flying to Vancouver and staying at the airport hotel before catching a cab to Squamish. Since we couldn't afford hotel rooms for the rest of the days, I had asked in advance on social media if anyone would be willing to let us crash at their home, and one very kind family with a nice, large basement and several air mattresses obliged. They even took us sightseeing in the mountains the next day, and during our outing, we were recognized by a couple of fans—the first time that had ever happened to me. It was my first time out of the country, and it was shaping up to be a memorable one.

The actual festival debut of A Motown Tribute to Nickelback was, indeed, one of the most memorable experiences of my life. Everything about it was exciting: our trailer, whose door was marked "A Motown Tribute to Nickelback"; the artist-only tent stocked with free snacks and beer; the pre-show sound check in which we pretended to know what we were doing ("Can I get a little more 1K in my monitor?") but really hadn't a clue. It was obvious to us that we'd been booked for our novelty value, but still, we felt like the mischievous upstarts who had somehow conned their way into the exclusive music world. If nothing else came out of this, we were thrilled just knowing that we'd succeeded in making some ridiculous idea debuted on the Internet come to life on a big stage for a night.

There were about a hundred and fifty people gathered before us at the start of our set. Not a robust showing, but significant nonetheless because each and every one of those hundred and fifty people was very obviously a fan...and we'd never seen A Motown Tribute to Nickelback fans before. One girl had even hand-lettered a very attention-grabbing, oversized "I LOVE YOU TAMBOURINE GUY!" sign, which, as you can imagine, sent Tim over the moon.

Something magical began to transpire as our set got under way. Right before our very eyes, the audience doubled, then doubled again, and then doubled again, until the energy emanating from the crowd had reached a fever pitch and everyone was singing along to us (well, to Nickelback, anyway). The high point of the show for us involved the tossing onstage of an article of intimate clothing by an adoring young lady during the appropriately titled song "Rockstar." It was insanity, and we were relishing every second of it.

We buzzed with the high from that performance for quite some time, even keeping our suits on after the set so that we could walk back and forth across the festival grounds and be recognizable to fans. There were a few post-show interviews given that probably should be destroyed, seeing as we were drunk on Canadian beer and fleeting fame. It was my first taste of the life of a successful touring musician, and at nearly thirty-one years of age, with a decade of trying to make it happen under my belt, it was intoxicating.

THE QUIET BIRTH OF POSTMODERN JUKEBOX

Contrary to popular belief, an "overnight success" has often been years in the making. In the same way that we're only able to see the tip of the iceberg that's above water, the general public really only gets to see the "overnight" part of a success story.

A truly successful project generally takes years to build and involves a series of smaller successes punctuated by a few failures. Eventually, a critical mass of attention is reached, and the project gets launched into the mainstream, where it circulates widely, and its identity is cemented in its current form—a form that, intentionally or otherwise, rarely pays obvious homage to the years of blood, sweat, tears, and more rudimentary sounds that engendered it. Such was the case for Postmodern Jukebox.

Around the time of our Motown Nickelback triumph, I had the idea for a YouTube series revolving around the creation of an alternate universe of covers of top Billboard hits, featuring a variety of guest musicians and vocalists. I didn't envision much structure to the format: Invite some friends over, shove a page of hastily penned sheet music into their hands, and hit Record. Often, I'd found, the simplest of formulas lead to the most exciting results.

Hearing Miche Braden add her masterful vocal style to my "Tainted Love" arrangement on *BioShock Infinite* had inspired me, and I was ready to start bringing vocalists and instrumentalists into my YouTube world. Naturally, I kept it in the family, and the musicians I selected for the first video all had been classmates of mine at Hartt: vocalist Emma Walker, saxophonist Ben Golder-Novick, bassist Chris Anderson (from both The Sesha Loop and Gordon Hunter & The Wandering Rocks), and harpist Brandee Younger. Scanning the Billboard Top 10, I settled on a song that seemed to have potential: "Paparazzi," a hit from the debut album of an up-and-coming artist named Lady Gaga. It had a pleasant minor key verse with a jazzy melody that would adapt well.

The shoot for the video was a laid-back affair. The gang showed up at my basement apartment and, after a lengthy ordeal involving the maneuvering of an unwieldy harp through a back alleyway rife with stray cats, we got to work. It was a pretty loose arrangement, even by my 2010 standards. I gave chord charts and vague instruction to aim for a quasi-Latin feel to Chris, Brandee, and Ben, and then we just kind of ran with it.

After recording, I synced the audio to the video on iMovie and placed a music video–style lower-third title in the bottom-right corner of the frame. I sat there for a minute as the cursor blinked, trying to think of a catchy name for this series. Finally, I had an idea that seemed good enough: I highlighted the text box and typed "Postmodern Jukebox."

"Postmodern Jukebox" felt like a placeholder at the time, but the more I thought about it, the more it seemed to fit the project I had in mind: *Postmodern* because it questioned the historical walls between genres and blended the old with the new, and *Jukebox* because it showcased pop songs that would be familiar to a lot of people. Of course, I had no idea if the name—or even the project—would stick for more than a couple weeks. All I knew was that it sounded smart, it was somewhat self-explanatory, and—most importantly—it would look cool on a t-shirt.

The first Postmodern Jukebox video received only a couple thousand views in its first week, but I believed that the concept had vast potential as a vehicle for collaboration with talented vocalists. The video I filmed soon after—a moody take on a new Rihanna song called "Only Girl" that featured Brandee's friend Niia on vocals—demonstrated this clearly. Smooth and mellow yet also pitch perfect, Niia's voice was stunning. I'd first heard her on another video she'd done with Brandee, and despite having already garnered worldwide recognition as the featured vocalist in Wyclef Jean's hit "Sweetest Girl," Niia was incredibly receptive to my invitation to collaborate on something more homegrown. We decided to meet up at a rehearsal studio in New York City and see if we could brainstorm some ideas.

Everything about Niia was unique, right down to her appearance. She was tall and slender, wearing a black, baggy sweatshirt, a large streak of dyed gray hair through her high ponytail. She was shy—an obvious introvert—but as she warmed up, she came to life, spilling forth creative visions of concept albums and charming, self-deprecating musings.

Niia was offered lots of record deals after singing on a platinum record at age eighteen, but she hadn't felt that any of them were the right fit for her—a self-described "weirdo" with a Frederic Chopin tattoo and an obsessive love for jazz and James Bond movies. I was struck by her ability to follow her vision so strongly at such a young age. While I could relate to feeling like an outsider, I knew nothing about having a record go platinum and *still* feeling that way. She wasn't interested in mainstream attention or being *cool*, Niia explained to me. She wanted to find her own voice as an artist and express it in ways that were intriguing to her. As I listened to Niia speak with such earnest conviction about her artistry and values, I knew I was in the presence of someone who would help inspire me to soar creatively, too.

Despite its rawness, maybe in part because of its rawness, "Only Girl" remains one of my favorite videos. We shot it in candlelight—Niia's idea—to make it look moody, but with my limited cinematography skills, it just came out dark and grainy. The audio, though, was another story, with a happier ending. The arrangement for "Only Girl" was the first I'd written in a more measured style, to complement a specific singer's vocals. The combined effect of harp, piano, cello, and Niia's voice was something magical, and it transformed the source material, a slightly raunchy Top 40 dance hit, entirely. Beyond that, it was also my first time recording a "serious" cover. There was no viral hook to this track, just a heartfelt performance by an intensely creative singer, set to a unique arrangement.

Niia and I collaborated quite a bit in those days, riffing on each other's energy, often spending hours talking about music and exchanging ideas for projects—*What if we did a show with a theremin player? What if we mashed up Nirvana and Katy Perry?* With Niia, these ideas were never simply all talk, either. When she stumbled upon an old woman playing a musical saw in the Times Square subway station, she wasted no time in inviting her to perform at one of her concerts (though it fell through due to the budget; who knew musical saw players command such high fees?). I produced some of her studio sessions and an orchestral concert of James Bond themes for her, and she sang on many of my videos, including my thirtieth birthday cover of "Imagine." Despite shunning the mainstream, Niia's talent and statuesque poise kept her in near constant demand for galas, launch parties, and other high-profile industry events, and we'd often play those together, delighting in the work but also in the people-watching.

No matter how many of these fancy gigs we did, we always felt like we were sneaking into a secret society. For one particularly elaborate gig, we were even provided private transportation... by aircraft. We snapped a lot of pictures and daydreamed about what it would be like to live like the wealthy.

"You're going to be wealthy someday," Niia pronounced. "I just know it. Just promise me you'll stay grounded."

I brushed aside her prediction. Producing a quirky YouTube channel hardly seemed like a recipe for wealth.

One day, in late 2011, Niia called to tell me that she'd been invited to sing at *Sleep No More*—a buzzy new immersive Off-Broadway experience playing in New York City—and that she wanted to bring me as her accompanist. I knew very little about the show, but I always enjoyed performing with Niia, so I didn't need to think twice before accepting. I threw on a cheap suit and tie and caught the train into the city to 34th Street.

Styled like an old nightclub from the 1930s, the Manderley Bar, with its red velvet interior and elegant round cocktail tables, was the "hotel bar" at the McKittrick Hotel—the faux-1930s hotel that housed the experience. Creepy taxidermy adorned the wall over a bar tended to by stylish, vintage-clad employees. In a dimly lit corner, a fortune teller read a guest's tarot cards while a pair of actors danced to the resident band's swing music. It was as though I'd stepped into a dreamscape, and I fell instantly in love with everything about it.

I don't remember what Niia and I played that night—so mesmerized and transported by the setting was I—but we must have made quite an impression on the producers, who hired us to perform every night for a week straight during their popular Halloween parties. This was a huge break for me, and so I treated myself to a new suit; it felt earned.

At the series of Halloween parties, we performed thirty-minute duos, consisting, for the most part, of mashups and hauntingly jazzy covers of pop songs. Our sets were almost entirely improvised, and the crowd was consistently enthusiastic. On one especially memorable night, Reggie Watts came onstage and jammed with us on a cover of the Talking Heads' "Psycho Killer." Another night, I announced to the audience that we would take anyone's cell phone and make a song from their most recent text message conversation—sung by Niia's pristine voice. This spontaneous party trick turned out to be such a huge hit that we began incorporating it into each performance, resulting in Grammy-worthy songs like "Grabbing a Taco" and "I'm Here, Where Are You?"

Seeing the *Sleep No More* show itself was a transformative experience for me. An immersive, self-guided extravaganza of dance and movement, staged throughout the more than one hundred rooms at the McKittrick, it was like nothing I'd ever seen. Instead of watching onstage action from a seated distance, the audience members—all clad in identical white masks—were free to explore the venue's five sprawling floors on their own, at whatever pace and in whichever order they desired. The space itself was meticulously designed to look, feel, and sound like the set of a Hitchcock movie—a 1939-era hotel with a sinister bent. So flawlessly orchestrated was the whole thing that, after moving through it, I found myself filled with a barely containable sense of possibility and humming with creative ideas. What I didn't know at the time was that soon enough, this mystical universe would grant me something even more priceless than it already had by way of merely existing: the creative license to produce any musical world I could imagine.

GETTING THE BAND
BACK TOGETHER

t was a few months after Halloween when Arthur Karpati, a
producer of the *Sleep No More* show, pulled me aside after
one of my now regular late-night piano sets at the Manderley
Bar. Not one to mince words, he flatly told me that he recognized
my talent as something special and wanted to figure out a way
to include me on the show's creative team. He suggested that we
create a position for me, a role that would task me with overseeing the group of musicians that performed throughout the night
in the Manderley Bar and at the various special events that were
hosted after the shows. I was getting a lot of work as a pianist at
the time, but I'd never held a salaried position in my life, and it
was industry knowledge that a well-paying, interesting gig like
this was extremely hard to come by—even for established talent. Furthermore, I saw the massive possibilities that came with
such a job: The show was a hot ticket, and I was bound to come
in contact with influential people who could help advance my
career, not to mention that I would be working among a whole
host of talented performers whose creativity and passion for the
arts would no doubt fuel my own. I told him to count me in,

and before I knew it, I was the music director of the hottest Off-Broadway show in New York City.

I came away from my tenure as music director at *Sleep No More* having learned a lot of valuable lessons. On the surface, I learned how to manage people—in particular, musicians with larger-than-life personalities. I learned the importance of giving clear directives in getting things done, how to delegate tasks to responsible people, and how to guide the collaborative process so that those involved are best equipped to make use of their talents and combine forces to produce great work. Although I later added a few of my friends to the talent roster—I favored the use of a rotating cast of musicians, as opposed to a fixed house band—I didn't have preexisting friendships with any of the musicians who were already in the show, and a couple of them tested their boundaries with me almost immediately. It bothered me at first, but eventually I learned that as long as I worked to contain my ego and avoid taking personally any professional issues that arose, it was possible to hold the line firmly while simultaneously showing respect to others. Having a big ego can be incredibly destructive when you're in a position of authority because it essentially broadcasts all your insecurities to the people you're supposed to be leading. To manage effectively, you must develop the ability to stay calm and unreactive at all times.

Creatively I learned a ton, even just by watching the show again and again and seeing how the individual pieces came together. One of my biggest takeaways was the realization that, when you create art, not everything has to make perfect or logical sense to the audience. In fact, an artistic production can be most interesting when its most surprising juxtapositions go unexplained. The narrative in *Sleep No More* was, at its core, a retelling of Shakespeare's *Macbeth* set in 1939 Scotland, but the play wasn't a period piece; it incorporated characters and themes from Hitchcock films, stylistic elements from David Lynch films, and, in one scene, samples of electronic dance music. The mixing of all these influences resulted in a work that is, without question, more dynamic and provocative than any number of "modern" adaptations of Shakespeare. It was tough to describe, and that was in part what made it so compelling.

A big part of my job was scouting for new talent, which put me in touch with several musicians who would, down the line, come to play pivotal roles in my YouTube channel's success as well. Two singers, Annie Goodchild and Karen Marie, were both performing in the show before I entered the mix, and right off the bat, their talents were apparent to me. Annie's distinctive, soulful voice was a perfect blend of jazz and R&B sensibilities, and Karen was a powerhouse vocalist and simply one of the most entertaining performers I've ever seen; she could captivate a room of four people as easily as she could a theatre of a thousand. After running an open call audition, I hired two more excellent performers: Ashley Stroud, a singer and dancer who exhibited perfect control over her smooth voice; and Cristina Gatti, a young actress whose brassy voice seemed to have come straight out of the 1940s, despite the fact that she had no prior experience and had never trained formally.

One evening, following one of my late-night mashup piano performances at the Manderley, a young woman came forward to compliment me on my "transpositional skills." She was beautiful, and a few minutes of conversation revealed that she also possessed a quick wit and a bubbly personality. We exchanged numbers, and the following week I took her on a date to a local dive bar. (I was no longer poor, but when it came to dating, I was still very cheap.) Her name was Robyn, and she knew about "transpositional skills" because she was *secretly* a singer herself.

Although Robyn had been singing for most of her life, she'd given little thought to actually performing in public; she was happy in her current job, working at a nonprofit that helped refugees find jobs. We soon began dating and occasionally wound up doing karaoke at local bars. My performances were generally jokingly over-the-top renditions of '80s power ballads that may or may not have involved me removing my shirt, but her antics-free performances consistently stole the show. I was a little surprised that she never tried to pick up singing gigs on the side, but I didn't press the subject. I got it; she didn't want to be thought of as a cliché, as just another aspiring singer with a day job in New York City.

Corralling all the *Sleep No More* musicians—each of whom had unique tastes and aims—into giving great performances gave me perspective on how to manage my own artistic priorities. I could see how people's passions for certain kinds of music were what made them great musicians, and watching their passions emerge and evolve was a great reminder to me not to leave my own by the wayside.

The new job at *Sleep No More* kept me busy, and the steady income allowed me to move out of Agatha's basement and into a nicer building a few blocks down with stainless steel appliances (including a stove, which was still a novel concept to me) and a view of the New York City skyline. In some ways, my life had become more stable and comfortable than ever before, but, wary of not letting my own unique passions get sidelined, and aware of how important it was that I keep actively developing them, I felt the itch to resume making videos in my new place.

One night, I was taking audience requests on my slightly buggy, TEDx-featured streaming site *Emote CTRL*, sitting on the couch in my new apartment, with my red keyboard facing the laptop camera. Robyn, who had by now officially become my girlfriend, was with me, and I wanted to give her a chance to sing in a low-pressure setting. She took to it instantly. We had the online chat audience requesting songs flipped into different genres and Robyn singing continuously while I turned the songs into ragtime, reggae, and other styles on the piano. She was quick at following the changes and would often come up with funny and witty ways to highlight the new genres. The audiences loved her, and she was loving performing for them. One request that came through the chat feed that initially stumped us both was " 'Thrift Shop' as ragtime." Neither of us had heard of the Macklemore song "Thrift Shop" that was currently climbing the charts, but we could tell by the repeated requests for it—all by different viewers—that this song was destined to be popular. I pulled up a recording of it online, and we listened to it once through to get a feel for it. Then, embracing the kind of close audience feedback that had helped spark previous success, I began playing a ragtime version of the sax riff while Robyn sang the lyrics in a jazzy manner. The chat feed went crazy.

The impromptu jam on "Thrift Shop" was so compelling, in fact, that I decided I would use it to restart my Postmodern Jukebox series on YouTube, which had been languishing since I'd started my full-time job at *Sleep No More*. I imagined giving it a full hot jazz treatment, with piano, upright bass, and drums.

"That's cool! Which singer are you going to get to sing it?" Robyn asked, when I shared the idea.

I pointed at her. She seemed taken aback.

"Me? Why don't you use one of the professional singers you work with? They're amazing! No, I don't think I'm ready to do this."

"You are definitely ready. Trust me, it's going to come out great."

"No....I'm not a real singer. I don't really know jazz—or whatever. I listen to Ke$ha."

Robyn had a knack for self-deprecation, but managing the *Sleep No More* musicians had given me a strong gut feeling for when someone was and wasn't up to a task, and most of it had to do with their commitment. Even if she was reluctant to admit it, I could tell that Robyn wanted to do this badly. And so I called her out.

"You're doing this because you know you'll regret it if you don't. Don't be a coward. Don't be a *perfectionist*."

She rolled her eyes, all too familiar with my tendency to get preachy about perfectionism.

"Okay, Scott Bradlee," she said, gently mocking me. "I'll learn it. But if I don't do good, I'm going to cry."

Robyn turned out to be a quick study and came up with some really great phrasing for the lyrics. Her melody was evocative of a lot of late 1930s swing tunes, so I threw in a middle section that loosely quoted Louis Prima's 1936 staple "Sing, Sing, Sing." Once we had it roughly figured out, I called up Adam and Allan and set up a time for us to record. I dragged my microphones and studio gear—my ever-constant reminder of my own personal credit crisis of '05—out of my storage closet and pushed aside the living room sofa to make room for us to set up shop.

Still new to bourgeois apartment life, I was afraid that my new neighbors might not appreciate the blare of a full band, so I decided to keep it low volume by stripping down the drum set to a single snare and by not amplifying Adam's upright bass. I positioned the camera on a tripod facing the plain white wall of the living room. We had just enough space for Allan's snare drum, Adam's bass, my bright red keyboard, and, in the corner, for Robyn, who wore a vintage-inspired dress and a flower in her hair. After a bit of rehearsal, I hit the Record button on both my computer and the camera, then gingerly climbed back into the cramped space behind my keyboard to count off the song.

I'm gonna pop some tags
Only got twenty dollars in my pocket...

We were off to the races and settling into a nice groove, if a bit of a quick one, given the sheer number of words in the song. Adam and Allan gave a few playful "gentlemanly" nods to one another throughout, and Robyn did her own approximation of how she thought singers from that era moved their hands (what YouTube viewers later called "washing an invisible car"). It was a really fun arrangement to play, and for me it felt especially good to be recording again.

The session went smoothly, and afterward, I bought falafel sandwiches for everyone—my go-to form of compensation in those days for the musicians I collaborated with on YouTube. I already knew that what we'd just recorded was quality work, but after everyone left and I sat down to listen to it, it occurred to me that we may have caught lightning in a bottle. Only time would tell.

I did my best to prepare Robyn for her YouTube debut by explaining that some websites might share the video, and some commentators on those sites might leave nasty comments. I told her that it was very likely the video could get upward of ten thousand views—which was a bit hard for her to fathom—and that the only downside to it going viral would be that some people get their kicks from publicly deriding anything that's currently trending. She didn't seem too concerned, though.

"I'll be fine, it's only the Internet," she assured me. "It's not real life."

From the instant I shared the video to my Facebook page, I had an inkling that it was going to be a success, but I had no idea just *how* successful it would prove to be. The video was getting a tremendous number of shares, and people all over the world were telling their Facebook friends about this "vintage" cover of "Thrift Shop" that they *had* to see. I went to bed that night satisfied that I'd done my job and confident that the video was bound to rack up ten thousand more views by morning.

I was off in my estimate by a factor of ten: Instead of ten thousand views, it had racked up one hundred thousand *and* earned itself a spot on the front page of Reddit. The video was getting tweeted several times a minute, and it had already spread to influential websites like *Huffington Post*. We were billed, alternately, as The Postmodern Jukebox Band or ScottBradleeLovesYa, depending on how hastily the author of the post had checked the facts. When I woke up, I had several texts from a very panicked Robyn, who had stumbled on the Reddit thread and discovered a smattering of unkind reviews of her performance among the positive ones. She hadn't been as prepared for the nastiness of the Internet as she'd thought she'd been, and that's understandable. It's one thing, as an artist, to brace yourself mentally for potential negative reception of your work. Actually experiencing it, though, can hurt like hell, especially the first few times you put an act of creative expression—a part of yourself—out into the world. Convinced that she had failed, Robyn was in tears. Obviously, she had not failed, and I offered to take down the video if it was upsetting her that much. She said no, though, that she'd be okay.

I breathed a sigh of relief. I was very glad she'd said that because it looked like Postmodern Jukebox was about to break the Internet.

Our "vintage" cover of "Thrift Shop" went on to receive a million views in just a week's time. On the day after its release, it was the third most viewed video on all of YouTube. It felt so surreal to see a still image of ourselves on the site, right up there with some of the biggest celebrities. Robyn would send me screenshots of different funny comments and emails that she received; she enjoyed the fan mail and would always try to write back. My inbox, meanwhile, was overflowing with requests, well-wishes, and inquiries from people wanting to hire our band—which was slightly problematic, since Postmodern Jukebox was, to me, a video series, not a band. Thus began the long, winding journey of attempting to define what exactly Postmodern Jukebox *is*.

As is the case whenever a project gains traction, the smartest thing I could do right then was to keep going.

HOW I LEARNED TO STOP WORRYING AND LOVE MY YOUTUBE TROLLS

So have you read the comments on 'Don't You Worry Child'?"

"Not really, why?" I cringed, afraid that Robyn had stumbled across another negative one that might ruin her day. She was still very new to the whole performing thing.

"Lots of people say I look like someone named Sasha Grey. So...I looked her up, and she's a porn star."

"Oh jeez, people say crazy stuff. Are you upset about that?"

"No," she smiled. "She's really pretty! So I'm okay with it. Well, other than seeing a few things when I was Googling her that I now can't unsee."

I was becoming all too familiar with the phenomenon that is the YouTube comments section. It was—and still is—a strange, sometimes ruthless place where you can observe our society slowly learning to get used to madness born out of the collusion of anonymity, freedom of speech, and the ability to say something to the entire world at once. Before the Internet, most people didn't have to go through life reading vile insults directed at them on a daily basis, a phenomenon that is now familiar to most

artists who release material digitally. And although reading negative or even downright cruel comments may initially prove disheartening, it's not necessarily a bad exercise for an artist looking
to develop a thick skin.

An incredibly small percentage of YouTube viewers will take
the time to comment on a video, even if it's absolutely their favorite video. Sure, the more invested viewers might give it a "like"
or a share, but the vast majority simply watch it and then continue on with their day. Of the small percentage of viewers who
do choose to comment, there are likely to be some who enjoy
expressing contrarian points of view or who take malicious pleasure in undercutting another person's accomplishments. These, in
sum, are your proverbial haters, and there's not much you can do
to stop them from hating, short of banning everyone and anyone
from leaving comments. And while I did, at times, contemplate
doing just that, I soon learned that engagement from the haters
often actually *strengthened* and *mobilized* our fan base.

I began to think of the YouTube comments section as its own
strange ecosystem, full of diverse organisms interacting with one
another in ways that, intentionally or unintentionally, influenced
the health and growth of the system itself. Here's a rundown of
just a few of the organisms I observed:

Cheerleaders—Always positive and enthusiastic, as the name
implies. Providers of unwavering support and happy vibes,
cheerleaders are often the first to comment; their upbeat feedback nicely primes your other viewers to follow up with their
own notes of appreciation.

Critics—Often people who self-identify as fans, though you
only hear from them when they don't like something. They
generally avoid knee-jerk hateful comments and try to maintain a standard of objectivity in their criticisms. When their

comments are spot-on, critics can provide precious insight into your blind spots. When their comments focus more on pointing out mistakes and weaknesses that you're aware of already, critics can prove even more frustrating than outright trolls. This is especially true if you're someone with a recently tamed perfectionist streak.

Advocates—Although they do on occasion write positive, thoughtful messages of support, advocates are more frequently found offering rebuttals to critics that demonstrate substantial knowledge about the content's creator. Cultivating a strong fan base among this breed of commenter can prove handy, as advocates will reliably jump in to explain and defend your work when discussion in the comments section becomes heated—which spares you the trouble of doing so yourself (note: avoid doing so at all costs if you value your sanity).

Professors—The authors of what are by far the longest comments, often sharing "inside" information and/or historical perspective on a video. Their primary goal is to educate others, although they will, on occasion, write gratuitously long essays as rebuttals to critics.

Parasites—Known for commenting with expressions of support that double as thinly veiled pleas for others to watch their own videos. It's an age-old strategy to get more attention, but hey, I've been there, so I can't really knock the hustle.

Comics—The purveyors of the clever one-liners that get the most up votes, usually rendering them top comment. Comics seem like fun people, and their humor helps keep others on your page longer, which translates to more watch time on your videos.

Trolls—The proverbial haters who are "gonna hate." Trolls' comments are generally so outlandish as to be laughable. The impulse may be to block them, but if you let your advocates go after them instead, you'll find that the ongoing conflict continues to bring those locked in the debate back to your video and page, thereby keeping engagement high and the discussion alive.

The typical pattern for our early Postmodern Jukebox videos commenced with the Cheerleaders leading the pack out of the gate (often declaring "First!" in the process), followed by a couple Critics, once they'd had time to formulate their argument, chiming in to make a case for why the video was actually, "meh, not your best work." This then led to the beginnings of a subthread comment war, as Advocates rushed in to tell the Critics why they were wrong. Often, both sides would lose their tempers, and the attacks become increasingly personal. In the midst of all the distracting subdrama, a Comic would find just enough cover to sneak in and submit the perfect one-liner that would begin to accumulate up votes. As the view count grew, a Troll might wander by to offer a concise and under-punctuated "you suck just give up." The next day, a Professor would pontificate on the video's true intent to the masses and provide detailed biographical information on every person who took part in the video. For some reason, whatever he says will likely get marked as spam.

Really, it's all a bit of madness, and initially it seems like an awful thing to have to deal with. However, this commenting eco-system plays an important role in building a following. You *want* haters; when there are haters, your following bands together and becomes even more loyal to you. If you don't have haters, despair not. It only means that not enough people have seen your work yet. Look forward to the day when you do finally get the haters you've been waiting for and can thank them for taking time out of their busy schedules to help generate more views and discussion on your video. Or, do as I've done on a few occasions and offer them an obviously over-the-top apology with a promise to "try harder," followed by a link to a generic-looking "FREE Chili Lime Wings!" coupon you found on Google image search. There's just no way to answer that.

For those of you still troubled by the terribleness of most website comments sections, I can offer my reassurance that the overall trend online seems to be moving away from anonymous posting and increasingly toward the linking of comments with actual individuals. Presumably, this will encourage people to interact more civilly with one another online. In the meantime, however, it's best to develop a thick skin and view the whole circus with detached amusement and an appreciation for what said circus can do for you. Robyn perhaps never got completely used to reading comments like "singer looks like bitch," but she did eventually devise her own solution to feeling at the mercy of the comments section's sometimes cruelty—by stopping reading the comments altogether.

While my YouTube fans and trolls were busy at each other's throats, I was hard at work, trying to follow the success of "Thrift Shop" with another video that would further cement our viral credentials. This next Postmodern Jukebox video spotlighted another current pop song: Ke$ha's club anthem "Die Young." Recalling my years as Motown Nickelback Guy, I was somewhat worried that releasing another jazz-influenced video could pigeonhole the group, so we called on Robyn's ability to mimic a country-and-western twang and the talents of our violinist friend David Wong to give the arrangement an old-time country twist. It was a simple video, but then again, we weren't trying to reinvent the wheel; we just wanted to put out another entertaining song remake—in this case, it was "Ke$ha Gone Country."

THE INTERNET
AS AMPLIFIER

Ever since my very first video went viral, I had looked to understand which websites could be used in coordination with YouTube to best help my future videos make a splash. I had spent a couple weeks studying the inner workings of Reddit—the site of user-curated links that was undoubtedly responsible for the killer viral spread of "Thrift Shop"—and trying to pick out some of the repeat characteristics of successful posts. One thing that seemed to be in our favor was the fact that the denizens of Reddit—"redditors"—seemed to prefer the kind of guerrilla-style, low-budget, single-camera videos I made over slicker productions. There was also a tendency to root for the underdog on Reddit—something we could use to our advantage.

When it came time to launch the "Die Young" video, I threw up a shamelessly Reddit-friendly title on the post: "I had a couple of hours free yesterday, so I invited some friends over to do a Country remake of a Ke$ha song. Let me know what you think." Given that the post's title was what people saw first on Reddit, it needed to be eminently clickable, enticing in what it promised to deliver while also appealing to the website's community in their own voice. I would spend hours coming up with potential titles, running them by Robyn and "Die Young" violinist David Wong, another Reddit aficionado. This was before the term *clickbait* exploded in popularity and application, but there's no question that the DIY strategy I was employing at the time was remarkably similar in principle. In any case, it worked, and I felt confident doing it because I knew we at least had great content to back it up.

Since my subscriber count on YouTube was still small, making it to the front page of a huge site like Reddit was akin to hitting the jackpot; achieving that alone could very quickly get us upward of two hundred thousand additional views. From there, YouTube's ranking algorithm took care of most of the promotion for us, automatically identifying such a video as "viral" and then highlighting it site-wide.

Our new video was met with grumbling from a few redditors who (correctly) saw us as having greater, more commercial ambitions than simply jamming in my apartment. Their gripes and our true intentions aside, the post shot to the front page once again, securing us another viral hit. This was huge; it's rare to achieve viral success at all, and it's rarer still to repeat that success. My YouTube subscriber base was rapidly expanding, now passing thirty thousand, and requests and song suggestions were coming through nonstop. Fans seemed to be taking to our model of translating current pop songs into vintage genres quite readily, and they were also demonstrating a willingness to purchase (not even illegally download!) our music wherever and whenever we made it available. In her very first interview, Robyn—when asked to name her favorite jazz singer—responded with, "Probably Ke$ha."

Our fame was clearly on the rise. It was time, I decided, to produce an EP that would announce to the world that Postmodern Jukebox was a legitimate musical act.

MAKING IT ON A BUDGET

Introducing Postmodern Jukebox may have been the lowest-budget album that charted in 2013. Everything, from the cover art (a photo of Adam, Allan, Robyn, and me, taken using the self-timer on my camera) to the recording process (live, one-take recordings that I engineered, mixed, and mastered myself), went against what a record label—no matter how small—would generally agree to release. The levels were frequently inconsistent, since I didn't use monitors and played on my keyboard instead of a real acoustic piano. On one track, you can even detect the hum of an air conditioner in the background. Even so, I knew releasing entertaining content was more important than repeatedly polishing something that I would likely never feel satisfied calling complete anyway. I managed to find a small distributor that could get the album on iTunes and other outlets, and before long, we had our first EP out in the world.

The EP featured "Thrift Shop" and "Die Young," new remakes of Swedish House Mafia's "Don't You Worry Child" and Justin Bieber's "Beauty and a Beat," and an "electro-swing" remix of "Thrift Shop" produced by French DJs Bart & Baker. I also included two "bonus tracks": alternate versions of a couple of the songs, digitally aged to sound as though they were recorded on turn-of-the-century phonographs, à la *BioShock Infinite*. With minimal instrumentation consisting of just my Nord keyboard, Adam's upright bass, Allan's snare drum, a horn or two, and Robyn's voice, the new songs perpetuated the "modern pop-as-vintage jazz" trend we had been cultivating.

The EP qualified as both a live album *and* a studio album because we shot videos to go along with every single live-recorded track. No overdubs were used, and every track was recorded simultaneously in my living room on an 8-track setup. I didn't even hire an outside engineer; I would press Record on my laptop and my Canon 60D camera and then scurry back to my place at the keyboard to count off the band. There were no monitors for the vocal mic, either, so a lot of the time poor Robyn could barely hear herself. To render the videos more entertaining than your standard studio session fare, we incorporated sight gags and played to the camera, letting our sense of humor shine and the fun we were having show. Each session, of course, ended with an order for falafel sandwiches, usually from Pita Pan, a restaurant in Astoria with a ridiculous website that played pita-themed drum and bass while you perused the menu.

Introducing peaked at number two on the iTunes jazz charts in the week of its release, supplanting many conventional jazz artists and evergreen recordings in the process. I was shocked and very excited. This was before my enthusiasm was tempered by my learning that jazz was the lowest-selling category on iTunes, but even so, it was an accomplishment. The key to our success—I was sure of it—was the videos; I positioned links alongside each video to drive traffic to the album, so each individual video was effectively an additional opportunity to boost album sales. The "Thrift Shop" remix proved unexpectedly popular internationally; it became a top-ten hit in Hungary, and the video I made for it—a series of public domain performance clips of Cab Calloway cut to fit the music by way of digital editing—was featured on a popular movie review site over there. A firm believer in being accessible to my fans and showing love for *their* love for us, I tried my best to answer as much Hungarian fan mail as possible (thanks, Google Translate!).

Thus was established the Postmodern Jukebox formula for album releases: release a bunch of videos as singles, then repackage them together as an album and add a few new tracks to draw the release period out over the course of about a month, rolling out new videos each week. To me, this release schedule continues to make sense for Internet-based music acts, and it feels much more natural than going into a studio every couple years to slave away on one painstakingly considered album. Times have changed, and the definition of an "album"—once typically reserved for the long-playing record—should probably be changing with them. My thinking went something like this: We don't use records anymore, so why persist in making albums based on that tradition if most people are simply going to purchase (or stream) only their favorite singles anyway? I've always enjoyed the challenge of tailoring my creative output to new media, so the decline of album sales following the advent of digital music formats hasn't troubled me all that much. Just spend less money making the albums and release more songs, and it all evens out. That's my philosophy, at least, and it will be for as long as it keeps proving successful.

At the time of the EP's release, most industry people had a hard time wrapping their heads around what I was doing. When *Billboard* contacted me to ask for a photo credit on our album cover, I wrote back, "Photo by camera self-timer"; Billboard reps asked me twice to clarify this statement. A number of video production companies contacted me, trying to sell me on services that would "take my music videos to the next level." They seemed perplexed when I assured them that we were precisely as hi-fi as we wanted to be, thank you very much. There was a charm to what we were doing—I felt it; our fans clearly appreciated it— and I wanted to maintain that DIY ethos for as long as possible and stay the scrappy underdog. Postmodern Jukebox felt to me like an Internet secret, seemingly known only to a select group of vintage music fans and the occasional very vocal hater.

In one day, all that changed.

HOW TO GO
MAINSTREAM—WITH THE
HELP OF MILEY CYRUS

I t was 9 a.m., and I was sitting at the newly purchased piano in my apartment, but I wasn't playing. Instead, I was talking to an ABC *World News Tonight* correspondent. Behind him was a camera crew, and next to them, in my cramped kitchen that hosted a prominently placed, Costco-sized bulk container of Quaker Oats, was a lighting rig. I imagined my neighbors assuming there'd been some crime committed as they witnessed all the commotion in the hallway caused by the crew's arrival.

Fortunately, the only crime being committed here was, arguably, of musical variety: getting four million views in a day on a doo-wop version of a controversial Miley Cyrus song. We'd just gone mainstream, and the media wanted to know what this whole Postmodern Jukebox thing was about.

By September 2013, we had built a core following of online fans who loyally tuned in every time we released something new. I had learned to work Reddit somewhat reliably and had been able to solicit consistent funding through Patreon, a brilliant, groundbreaking crowdfunding site started by another popular

YouTube musician, Jack Conte of Pomplamoose. Between this and the money I received from my work on *BioShock Infinite*, I had enough saved up to purchase a real piano, a used Yamaha G2 grand. Forever, I had dreamed of someday owning the real thing; that I was able to make this dream come true felt like a true career—and life—milestone. Confession: The day it was delivered, I slept on the couch next to it.

We had come up with some new pop songs we wanted to remake, including Carly Rae Jepsen's "Call Me Maybe" and K-pop star Psy's novelty hit "Gentleman." No longer camera shy, Robyn was enjoying the challenge of approximating many different vocal styles. I continued to give a genre description in the title of each video, such as "Vintage 1920s Gatsby-style" or "Vintage 1940s Swing" to give the viewer a frame of reference. Some of our critics took issue with this, complaining that it didn't sound period-authentic, but I was already past caring what the "jazz police" thought; we had something that worked, and it worked well. But my real ace in the hole was something I had been sitting on, waiting for just the right time to play: an NYC doo-wop group named The Tee-Tones.

The Tee-Tones were another Niia subway station find from a year earlier. Listening to them sing "Under the Boardwalk," she found herself captivated by their rough-and-ready harmonies and street corner sensibilities. Niia may have been an introvert, but she was incredibly bold when she saw performers who inter-ested her, and just as she had with the musical saw virtuoso, she invited the group to join her on a show at *Sleep No More*. They eagerly accepted, and Niia called me to break the news of her latest project.

"I met these doo-wop dudes, they're really dope. Can you help me put together a show with them? Like doo-wop stuff but modern and maybe some weird dark jazz vibes, too."

I knew exactly the sound she was looking for. "Of course," I said.

The Tee-Tones were a lively bunch. Then ranging in age from mid-forties to sixties, they became kids in a candy store upon entering the set of *Sleep No More,* playing with the props and cracking jokes as the stewards and managers observed nervously. The Tee-Tones could be ragtag, but they had heart and the kind of authenticity that just cannot be faked or taught. I began to pick up some of the terminology they employed for learning harmonies—a "drop" was when a major chord became minor, for instance—and found that their instincts were really great, despite a lack of formal musical training. My impulse was to compose the harmony lines myself, but it was better, I realized, to let them come up with their own in this case.

I was learning that part of being a good music director is being able to put aside the desire to control the output and allow others the opportunity to do what they excel at doing. It seems like a simple concept, but in practice, it can be a difficult experience—particularly for the ego—to permit things to drift away from your original vision and assume a more collaborative format. Give others a chance, and you just may find yourself surprised—and your ego rightfully humbled. The fact of the matter is that all great projects are collaborations; it's up to the person in charge to guide the process in a positive and fruitful manner. My tenure with *Sleep No More* helped me become fairly competent at this, although time would prove that I still had much to learn.

These were the considerations in my mind a year later, when the six of us—Robyn, Chip, bassist Aaron Wright, and Gerard Giddens and Scout Ford from The Tee-Tones—gathered in my apartment to remake Miley Cyrus' "We Can't Stop." The song had achieved a particular degree of notoriety, not just from its success on the Billboard charts and its bizarre, surrealist video but also from Cyrus' raunchy performance of it at the MTV Video Music Awards. I had already planned to cover the song as '50s doo-wop by the time we gathered to record the video, but this recent taboo drama surrounding it solidified the idea. After all, what's more sanitized than '50s doo-wop, and what needed to be sanitized more, apparently, than Miley Cyrus?

The session went smoothly. Robyn's lyrical take on the song's melody showcased her voice extremely well. Gerard and Scout came up with the titular echo in the choruses, which became something of a signature moment of the cover. I had even purchased a brand-new tube microphone from Guitar Center (which I returned the next day...old habits die hard) to add some analog warmth to The Tee-Tones' vocals. Listening to the recording for the first time, I knew we had a winner. It was a glorious recording, and its timeliness couldn't have been better. With the headline "After the VMAs, we decided to class up Miley Cyrus' 'We Can't Stop,' with the help of some doo-wop singers I met on the NYC subway," I posted the link to Reddit. The response right out of the gate was amazing. Even our detractors, who usually appeared in the threads to denigrate our work as "mediocre," were noticeably absent, and those who did show up were, dare I say, begrudgingly supportive. I released the video to Facebook simultaneously, and shares from people of all walks of life began rolling in. The post quickly got voted to the front page of Reddit, where it stayed for quite a while. Then something extraordinary happened.

I woke up the next day to a voicemail and emails from both ABC's *World News Tonight* and *Good Morning America*. I checked the view count on YouTube, and there, on the front page, was our video. The video was already fast approaching a million views, and it would go on to receive another three million by the end of the day. Comments ranged from overwhelmingly enthusiastic to downright vile—in a variety of languages. On September 4, 2013, our version of "We Can't Stop" was the most-watched video of all the billions of videos on YouTube.

And that was how ABC *World News Tonight* had ended up in my kitchen. They had been one of a few television shows to reach out in the wake of our video, asking if they could come to our studio. I invited the crew over to my apartment, which was much smaller and much less studio-like than they'd anticipated. They were pros, however, and managed to set up very quickly, just in time for the arrival of the segment's host.

The interview went pretty much as expected. Since it was traditional media covering YouTube, many of the questions were about money and whether I realized how lucky I was to be able to do this from my living room. I could tell they wanted at least an *appearance* of an overnight success story that would grab people's attention. I dodged most of the questions about money—traditional media was still shocked to hear that YouTubers could earn a living—but played along enough to give them good television. In the end, it didn't matter; we got bumped from the final broadcast, and the segment never aired. It was all right, though; we were already booked to perform on *Good Morning America*, television's top-rated morning show, in two weeks.

I felt a lot of pressure in that two-week lead-up. I had convinced myself that this was a make-or-break moment for Postmodern Jukebox, and I wanted to do everything I could to make it a success. Not only were we booked for an on-air featured performance, but we were also going to be presented as the "house band" that day, playing the show in and out of commercials and generally hanging out on set before returning to our regularly scheduled lives—by limo, of course. It was going to mean massive exposure for us and a chance for me to debut the idea of Postmodern Jukebox to the world.

I set about assembling my "dream team": Robyn, Adam, Chip, The Tee-Tones, a horn section, and violinist David Wong. I even had a few Postmodern Jukebox t-shirts screen printed so that I could give them to the hosts. Robyn, meanwhile, was a bit more realistic about the whole thing and was preparing for it as she had for any other video we'd done. She was anxious for it to be over, just so I would stop talking about it.

The producers knew they were taking a gamble by inviting an unknown, sort-of band from the Internet with no representation and a technical rider handwritten on a sheet of notebook paper to play on their respectable television program, so they decided to simultaneously invite dancers from a local dance school to perform in costume to our music, as a visual complement to our act.

In theory, this was a cool idea. Watching it back, though, it just looked plain weird. The costumes, selected to reflect certain songs in the medley—giant teddy bear backpacks as an homage to Miley's VMA performance, motorcycle helmets for Daft Punk's "Get Lucky"—probably were so subtle as to be meaningless to a good ninety percent of the show's television viewers. And, with no choreography—or even stylistic guidelines—the dancers were just freestyling collectively in a manner that could best be described as Brooklyn-warehouse-rave-meets-zombie-parade. Even worse, they received much more camera time than our band did. There are a couple of clear moments in the video that just perfectly capture our dismay at the scene unfolding before us; you could see it in our body language in the brief shots of us.

Awkwardness aside, the entire performance went down largely without incident, and it was an overall positive first experience for us appearing on air. The hosts were kind and plugged us throughout the show. I wanted to present them with the freshly silkscreened t-shirts on air, but the producers, perhaps wisely, had prohibited me from ad-libbing. Up to this point, Robyn and I had been careful to keep our relationship a secret from the public, since the idea of inviting random people from around the world into our private lives wasn't exactly appealing to either of us. The host, however, decided to bring it up during my interview.

"So Robyn is your girlfriend?"

And there it was; the cat was out of the bag. I was caught off guard and for a brief second irritated—*What bearing did this have on my music?*—but I knew it would be easier to just have it out there than to make concerted efforts to keep anyone from finding out. Besides, I figured, couples in the entertainment industry work together all the time; how much drama could really result from it?

We wrapped up the show, climbed into our limo (which was actually a Lincoln Navigator; not everything in showbiz is as it seems), and breathed a sigh of relief. We had gone from playing songs in a small apartment in Queens to playing them on national TV before millions of viewers; it was all finally beginning to sink in, and it was still only morning. I took Robyn to Astor Bake Shop—our go-to breakfast place—to get pancakes and just decompress in general. But when we got there, Robyn began to cry; despite her expressed indifference to the appearance, it was a lot of pressure for her, and she felt the weight of my ambitions falling on her shoulders. On top of all that, she was kicking herself for this one note that she was convinced she'd sung poorly on air.

"I let you down," she said mournfully. "You shouldn't have used me to sing on TV. Now I've ruined your project."

I hated to see her hurting. She was truly fantastic, and I was proud of how well she'd been dealing with the mounting fame.

"The hardest part is over," I said, trying to reassure her. "We did it. From now on, it will all be smooth sailing." I kissed her forehead gently. "Someday, we'll look back at this day and just think, wow, what a crazy day that was."

She tried her best to muster a smile, as our phones buzzed with incoming messages of congratulations.

BUILDING THE RIGHT TEAM

There's a stereotype that creative people tend to be lone wolves who fiercely guard their creations, and I wouldn't say it's inaccurate. In an industry where talent is routinely discovered, commodified, used up, and discarded, it also isn't exactly surprising. Once an artist has reached a certain level of success, however, *refusing* to trust others can actually backfire horribly. History is littered with instances of ideas by lone-wolf inventors never seeing widespread adoption because of a stubborn refusal on the wolves' parts to let anyone else touch their work, lest they be exploited.

For a long, long time, I was your typical lone-wolf creator. I had such an intense connection to my project that the mere thought of allowing anyone else into the decision-making process felt like an invasion. I was happy enough acting as Postmodern Jukebox's manager, booking agent, publicist, art director, and, on one occasion—when I sent a phony letter to an event company that had stiffed us—even lawyer. I was learning a lot and doing it on my own terms. When it got overwhelming, I would just try to remind myself that I was living my dream, on my own terms. On some days, though—and these days were starting to

Me, at age 9, at the bus stop on the first day of school. I clearly look thrilled about this.

Goofing off during a photo shoot with my very first band, The Sesha Loop. From left to right: drummer Mike Lapke, me, bassist Chris Anderson.

Playing a post-college gig at The Spigot in Hartford with Adam (pictured with bass guitar) and Rook, who appears to be rapping.

Another weird gig I booked with my friends, this time after moving to New York City. From left to right: Rook in a bear suit, Steve Ujfalussy, Ben Golder-Novick, and me in a powdered wig.

Photo shoot for my first band to go viral, A Motown Tribute to Nickelback. I instructed everyone to look serious—except for Tambourine Guy.

A Motown Tribute to Nickelback takes the stage in British Columbia, at the Live at Squamish festival. We were shocked to learn that we had fans—some of whom even made signs.

ABC *World News Tonight* setting up to interview me, after the Postmodern Jukebox cover of "We Can't Stop" became the most-watched video on YouTube for a day. They were under the impression that they were coming to our "studio"; turns out they were actually coming to my kitchen.

Robyn and me, just before Postmodern Jukebox made its television debut on *Good Morning America.*

Postmodern Jukebox live in Prague in June 2014. I brought my trusted red keyboard on this European adventure, the first of our many tours abroad.

Signing a head in Amsterdam. My internal monologue at the time of this photo is clearly, "How did my life turn out this way?"

Playing a New York City homecoming show at Best Buy Theatre, with Puddles making a guest appearance.

Haley Reinhart, moments before filming "Habits," her Postmodern Jukebox debut.

Taking the cast bowling in Germany during our 2015 European tour.

Setting up our new studio at Bro Mountain.

Nicole Atkins, just before recording the Postmodern Jukebox version of "Heroes." The track went on to feature in a Heineken PSA that aired during the World Series.

Starting off 2016 with our biggest show yet at the Roundhouse in London, England.

The PMJ tour bus makes a pit stop at my childhood home in New Jersey to surprise my #1 fans: Mom and Dad (front and back in the center). My mom's reaction was priceless.

Setting up for our first video shoot at PMJ Manor. Our video sets had come a long way from my Queens, New York, basement.

Morgan, Haley, and Ariana perform "All About That Bass" live at Radio City Music Hall, New York City.

occur more regularly—the scope of the work felt unmanageable. I couldn't deny that wearing all those different hats was making me a bit dizzy.

Back when I was in music school, I naively believed there would come a day when I would "make it" and, from that point onward, be able to earn a great living playing music I loved, with no stress whatsoever. Truth be told, though, stress is an integral part of being successful. Even after achieving a rewarding career, expect the relatively simple stresses of being able to pay your bills to quickly be replaced by the more complex stresses of managing multiple projects and many different individuals. As Notorious B.I.G. once said, "Mo' money, mo' problems."

After our appearance on *Good Morning America*, Postmodern Jukebox began making forays into performing outside my living room and inside private events. Other than Robyn, all of us had gotten our starts as live performers, so the transition was relatively smooth. I had experience booking my own gigs as a pianist and putting together jazz combos for parties, so I felt pretty well equipped to pitch the project to prospective clients, draw up basic contracts, and hire musicians. I wasn't much of a negotiator and probably often undersold the project, but I was too caught up in the excitement of potentially making a thousand dollars on a single gig to even care. For the most part, I brought my own PA to events and ran sound at the same time, at no additional cost to the client. In keeping with my previous terms of engagement as a pianist, I required only a hundred-dollar deposit to hold the date. Through it all, I held on to my jobs at *Sleep No More* and Robert Restaurant and managed to still teach a few weekly piano lessons. There was no guarantee that our viral fame would last, and so even when I was running on fumes, I was reluctant to turn down any extra work.

As a group, we played galas for luxury brands, conventions

for multilevel marketing firms, and even a frat party at the University of Pennsylvania, a gig that lasted all of fifteen minutes, until campus police were called in to shut down the party. We didn't have many songs in our catalog, so our sets consisted of a couple jazz instrumentals, six or seven Postmodern Jukebox songs performed back to back, and whatever else we could come up with to fill the time.

One notable early gig was our appearance in 2013 at Worldcon, home of the Hugo Awards for science fiction. The event organizers didn't have much of a budget, and we barely made a dime when it was all said and done, but that trip was worth it just for the stories, which started with getting dropped off at a Holiday Inn Express only to find out that our room (we had one double room for the five of us) was actually in a different, even lower-budget Holiday Inn Express. From there, it only got better: Our rides to and from the convention center in San Antonio were courtesy of elderly volunteers who often missed our calls because they had fallen asleep. We performed for a small crowd of mostly octogenarians, who, I was happy to see, seemed to enjoy our unusual musical juxtapositions. The trip also gave me the opportunity to have interactions like this one:

ME: Where do you live?

WOMAN WEARING A *STAR TREK* UNIFORM: In space.

ME: Haha, oh like *Star Trek*, I get it . . .

WOMAN: No, actually in space. I live on the International Space Station.

ME: Oh, wow. Didn't mean to judge you.

ASTRONAUT WOMAN: It's okay.

As entertaining as these gigs were, we were still firmly in "musical ice sculpture" territory, where we were treated as background music. Part of that was due to the nature of playing for private events: We weren't there because the entire company was Postmodern Jukebox fans; we were there because the company was throwing a *Great Gatsby*–themed party and we fit the aesthetic. The gigs paid well compared to what I was used to earning as a non-Internet sensation but hardly enough to justify all the work that went into putting them together.

I was confident, though, that Postmodern Jukebox could thrive as a much bigger and multifaceted production. I imagined it existing as part of some idealized world that blurred the lines between classic and contemporary—complete with guest performers, comedy, and old-school glamour—a kind of a cross, if you will, between Cirque du Soleil and a vintage Comic-Con. What's more, the Postmodern Jukebox universe wouldn't operate like the superficial, image-driven, pop chart–centric culture of today; we'd celebrate authentic, mind-blowing talent and the hard work that goes into mastering an instrument and a multiplicity of genres. My ambitions were boundless, but I didn't have the first idea of how to make the transition from fun event band to true concert act. I had gone as far as I could on my own. And then, in late 2013, I opened my email to find this:

Hi Scott,
My name is Jaron Lowenstein. I'm an artist (formerly one half of "Evan and Jaron") turned talent manager and I'm a fan of what you're doing. I believe you've met my bro before (Evan, founder of StageIt) and I'd like to learn more about you and see if there is some way to work together in some capacity.

I'm not sure what may come of it, but all my life I've just followed what interests me and let the rest fall into place.

Hit me back if you're interested and I look forward to speaking with you.

Jaron

I'd received a fair amount of press by this point, including a great interview with Audie Cornish on NPR's *All Things Considered*, but this was my first serious inquiry about representation. As someone who valued the flexibility of managing everything myself, signing with a manager and ceding control wasn't something I'd given much thought to doing. But reasoning that there was nothing to lose, I agreed to take a call from Jaron, with the private goal of collecting as much information from him as possible that I could then turn around and use for myself.

I did wind up getting a ton of information, but that's mostly because he talked very fast.

"Hey, it's Jaron. This is Scott, right? So, I'm watching this video, it's like a fuckin' singing clown or something, and I'm just thinking to myself, '*Somebody* has some skill here.' Just everything—the arrangement, the placement of the background singers, the presentation—it's clear that everything had a reason, and a *master* was involved somewhere. And then I see the name 'Scott Bradlee' on the channel, and I watch another video, and I'm like, HOLY SHIT! *This* one is great, too. It's *completely* different, but it has the *same fingerprints*. It's a breath of fresh air, especially after seeing all the fucking garbage YouTube covers that exist."

Right from the start, I knew this guy was either brilliant or insane. Or possibly both. As I'd already learned from Evan, Jaron had had some brief experience as a pop star a decade ago, as half of Evan and Jaron. Later on, he released a chart-topping country hit on his own—a clever breakup song called "Pray for You." By his own description, he was a "one-hit wonder, twice." I started to explain to him the basic concept of Postmodern Jukebox but didn't make it very far before he cut in excitedly.

"Yeah yeah, it's a variety show," he said. "There's different singers, and everyone's dressed up like it's fucking *Great Gatsby*, and it's in a supper club, and maybe there's the girls handing out cigarettes, and there's like, a fucking *tiger* in a cage somewhere."

To my surprise, he not only already grasped how it all worked, he shared my big-picture live-show vision, too. Well, maybe up to the tiger. But regardless of his taste in entertainment and whether it involved the participation of wild animals, it was nonetheless clear to me that he had a passion for management and that we were equally fascinated by employing bold strategies that might seem counterintuitive on their surface.

Jaron offered to work with me on a per-gig basis to start—no contract, and he'd only take a commission on gigs if he added value to them. I figured it was worth a shot. If it didn't work out, I'd only be out a few hours of phone time and possibly whatever it cost to rent a tiger.

We struck a deal, and I sent him a brief history of where I came from musically, what I did for work, and what kind of press I had received. Armed with this information, he went back to several of the clients with whom I had outstanding contracts and doubled the "dogshit" (his word) fee on every one of them, simply by getting them insanely excited about our act. I couldn't believe it. Part of me was still thinking he might be a bit insane, but based on those results, maybe insane wasn't the worst thing to be. I decided that this was someone who could really help take Postmodern Jukebox to the next level.

Within a month, Jaron guided me in bringing on a business manager to handle my finances, a lawyer to look over my contracts, and a booking agency to secure shows and build a touring operation—International Creative Management Partners, or

ICM. It all happened so fast that it was a bit disorienting—one minute, I was a one-man operation in my living room, and the next I was discussing brand strategy with bigshot Hollywood agents. I didn't know much about the music industry, and I had to constantly interrupt meetings in order to ask questions so I could understand what on earth people were talking about. Terms like *guarantee* (the money an act was guaranteed to receive for a show, regardless of ticket sales) and *backend* (the money an act would receive if they sold more than a designated number of tickets) were foreign to me. I also learned some valuable (but perhaps less fun) lessons about paying commissions and how fees would get divided up among the team. I was now officially an owner of an incorporated business.

I wasn't sure where it all would lead, but one thing was certain: Everyone was incredibly excited about this project. I spent a week in Los Angeles, waking up each day to meet with the various members of the team that Jaron had assembled. Scott Mantell from ICM—who was then the key agent for no less than Beyoncé—was already on the phone with promoters from around the world, telling them about the new act he was developing and how it was going to revolutionize the music industry.

Robyn, Adam, and Allan came with me on this trip, which was initially built around an appearance on *Extra!* We stayed at the Safari Inn in Burbank, California, and took some time to survey our surroundings. It felt so utopian that it almost tipped into the realm of dystopia—a land of happy automatons brainwashed by yoga and sunshine.

We taped two performances for *Extra!* outside at Universal Studios, including a version of "Timber" that featured Tim Kubart—who happened to be in town at the same time—as Tambourine Guy. Afterward, we were instructed to sign autographs for the fans gathered behind the barriers. I soon learned, to my embarrassment, that they were not fans at all but tourists who happened to stumble onto a television taping and had their curiosity piqued. There were several awkward instances of my signing autographs for people only to have them thank me and then ask, quizzically, "Who are you again?"

We also met one of Jaron's friends, nine-time Grammy-nominated saxophonist Dave Koz, who carved out time to make a cameo on a couple Postmodern Jukebox videos filmed in Burbank that week: a 1930s version of "Careless Whisper" and a jazz treatment of the *Game of Thrones* theme. Dave played great and was a good sport about rolling with our crazy video ideas, which involved him popping up in a different part of the frame for "Careless Whisper" each time he played the famous sax riff. At one point, he was even crawling across the floor, army style, to move from one location in the frame to another. A veteran entertainer, he loved the concept and seemed to understand and appreciate the entertainment value of our frenetic performances.

It was a whirlwind of a week, and I left Burbank more excited about the project than ever before. It felt like I was on the cusp of something major, and the best part was how unlikely it all seemed: I was a thirty-two-year-old man with an act that turned pop songs into ragtime and jazz. Even after a few viral successes, I'd seriously doubted whether there would be room for an act like mine in the traditional music industry. I had always wanted to create a popular touring show, but I'd also mentally prepared myself for a life of YouTube videos and private events. Now, armed with a team of people working to support my vision, I felt unstoppable. When gigs came in, I no longer worried that we might get stiffed because I had a lawyer to ensure that we wouldn't. If a client didn't get back to me, Jaron would leave polite but incessant messages for them. If I had an idea, I knew the right person to help make it a reality. As nice as the independence of working solo may be, the power of the right team is undeniable. The hard work of building an act had only just begun, but luckily I wouldn't be alone in that work.

CONSTRUCTING A
DREAM FACTORY

All of my experience—from A Motown Tribute to Nickel-back to my antics with Alan Alda in Robert Restaurant—had taught me that a little humor and the occasional over-the-top performance are two powerful buttons that could be pushed to get noticed. As I scaled up my team, scaling up my performance antics, too, only seemed logical.

One day, I told Adam that I wanted to record a video with a saxophone that shoots fire out of the bell and that I wanted to do it…tomorrow.

"Okay," he said. "Can we finish by eight p.m.? I have to study for law school."

It was 2014, and the Postmodern Jukebox musicians were officially no longer fazed by the crazy shoots that transpired in my apartment.

Over the past few months, we had been slowly expanding the vocal talent that appeared in our videos, and I was excited to put the chief female vocalists of the group—Robyn and *Sleep No More* vocalists Cristina Gatti and Ashley Stroud—together in one video. I had written a '60s girl group–style rendition of Ellie Goulding's "Burn," and it featured a greater level of detail than any of the videos I'd previously produced. The vocals involved switching between doo-wop harmony parts, lead lines, and overlapping melodies, and Ashley had choreographed the movements to fit the era.

It was time to make this thing happen. The aforementioned "flame-o-phone" was an invention wielded by saxophonist Stefan Zeniuk of the band Gato Loco. Basically, it was a baritone saxophone rigged with a flamethrower, which enabled its player to shoot flames up to six feet high in sync with the music. It was a sight to behold, kind of like the marching band equivalent of an EDM laser light show. Stefan, a trained fire performer, was known to incorporate it into his own shows, doing things like inviting the audience to roast marshmallows by its flame. It was perfect for a song whose hook was "...and we're gonna let it burn, burn, burn."

I had few reservations about bringing a flaming wind instrument into my small Astoria apartment. We set up and rehearsed the video as we would any other, first doing a dry run without the flame-o-phone. Then we decided to record. On the first flame-laden take, the smoke detector went off. No big deal; I simply took out its batteries. We carried on, positioning Stefan in the very back by the door. The singers did a great job of ignoring the heat and fire behind them. (Look closely, though, at Adam, the musician closest to Stefan, and you'll see him visibly wincing every time the flames shoot out of the bell.) We filmed two takes and then got the flame-o-phone out of there as quickly as possible, before anyone could call the fire department or building management on us. It was just another day at the Dream Factory—Cristina's name for my small Astoria apartment's living room.

The Dream Factory was my latest laboratory, and its casual setup—a couch, a shag rug, and the piano that took up the rest of the room—was ideal for creative brainstorming. For an artist, tapping into creativity is kind of like catching a butterfly. If you chase it, it will elude you, so the best you can do is to position yourself in such a way that it's lured ever closer until it's within reach, and then—WHOOSH!—net it before it can escape. (I don't know that using a butterfly metaphor here is particularly creative, but that's beside the point.) Artists live in constant fear of losing the ability to tap into their creativity, and they often develop bizarre rituals to aid them in this struggle—everything from keeping recording devices bedside to meditating with low-frequency binaural tones. For me, maintaining a simple space and inviting creative performers over to hang out was enough.

One important rule at the Dream Factory was not to over-work ourselves or force ideas to come. I've learned that there's a certain amount of creativity I can access within myself each day. If I use it all at once, it's gone, and I need to recharge by doing mindless chores, getting some exercise, or watching reruns of MTV's *Jersey Shore* (seriously, don't judge). To get back into the creative groove, I need to be relaxed enough to allow my mind to drift, with no thought of deadlines or other obligations.

Of course, creativity usually needs something else, too, to flourish, and that something is what I call *creative hunger*. For me, it's the name for what happens when creativity is mixed with *profound inspiration*. If you aren't filled with creative hunger, then it's all too easy to put things off, rationalize that a project is too difficult to tackle, or decide that you would be just as content watching TV instead. Ambitious young people generally start off with a great deal of creative hunger, but as they age and experience tastes of success here and there, the drive has a way of dissipating. After you've got a hit under your belt, it's tempting to simply keep enjoying the fruits of the labor you've already harvested. If you want to stay at the top of your game, though, it's imperative that you stay hungry.

Thanks to the emerging possibility of being able to do Postmodern Jukebox full time and the anything-goes atmosphere we were cultivating in the Dream Factory, I closed out 2013 with a creative hunger like never before—even greater than any I'd had in my twenties. This was something else—an opportunity to build something great from an idea I'd been developing for years.

To push the limits of what was possible with Postmodern Jukebox production-wise, we needed to first expand our audience as much as humanly possible. Jaron and I agreed that the videos themselves would be our engine for driving awareness of Postmodern Jukebox to the point where we could tour. Touring, I'd come to understand, was the true litmus test for an Internet-based act and the only way to achieve legitimacy in the industry circles I had recently begun to travel.

After expanding the roster of vocalists so that we could execute a wider variety of genres, we filmed a Postmodern Jukebox 2013 year-end medley of pop hits, in collaboration with *Cosmopolitan* magazine. Finally, it felt like fans were beginning to get why I'd been describing Postmodern Jukebox as a "musical collective." In addition to Robyn, The Tee-Tones, and Tim Kubart's Tambourine Guy character, the medley introduced to our group *Sleep No More* vocalists Karen Marie, Andromeda Turre, and both Cristina and Ashley. It was a silly day, full of antics with sticky notes and copy machines, but the one-off video that came out of that day—with its rotating cast of singers and ever-changing genres and fashions—would go on to set the blueprint for the touring show that I hoped to build.

The videos we produced at the Dream Factory explored the myriad possibilities of pairing unique talent with the Postmodern Jukebox concept. My time at *Sleep No More* had given me the opportunity to cultivate the raw talents of several singers, and Cristina Gatti—the one with the least experience—had improved by leaps and bounds. I was very excited to debut her on my You-Tube channel and tell her story: In the span of a year, she had gone from never having performed in her life to becoming a star singer at *Sleep No More*. Her success as a performer, however, didn't seem to have had any impact on her chatty, frenetic personality...proof, I guess, that success need not render a person unrecognizable.

"Hey, you guys! I brought DOOOOUGH-NUUUTTSS!" she said, arriving to practice my latest swing arrangement of Beyoncé's "Drunk in Love." "Well, actually, I got McDonald's on the way, but I *couldn't* pass Dunkin' Donuts without going in! Is that bad? I don't think it's bad...OHH you guys *have* to try the spin class that I discovered—it's called SoulCycle, and it's *amazing*... is that a *dog* outside?? It sounded like a dog! Aww, *puppyyyyy*!"

Cristina's loquacious temperament may not have been dulled by her fast-rising star, but even that was overshadowed by her singular voice. Opening with the smoky jazz club lyric "I've been drinking," Cristina's voice on "Drunk in Love" didn't seem to emanate from her so much as magically crackle forth from a 1940s radio.

Our fans loved every second of it, but it wasn't just they that loved it.

A couple days later, I checked my phone and noticed that I had six unread messages from Cristina, which in and of itself wasn't anything out of the ordinary. I figured she'd probably found a YouTube video of a puppy skateboarding that she was very enthusiastic to share. I opened her texts.

"BEYONCE SHARED OUR VIDEO!!!! OMG OMG OMG IS THIS REAL LIFE!?!"

Wildly off the mark.

I checked and saw that, indeed, the Beyhive was storming our YouTube channel with support. Postmodern Jukebox and

Cristina had just been anointed by one of the biggest celebrities on the planet. The Dream Factory had produced another glowing star.

In contrast to Cristina's wild ebullience, Ashley Stroud was a calm and intelligent performer, exceptionally well trained in both singing and dancing. She saw the possibilities of Postmodern Jukebox as a platform, and she instinctively knew what our videos needed to realize them. Unlike the rest of us, Ashley had been in numerous stage productions and understood firsthand the importance of tight, rehearsed choreography and blocking. I wanted to make a Postmodern video that would highlight her versatility as a performer and the care she took in crafting a highly polished performance.

Ashley's dance students at a school in Brooklyn introduced her to Iggy Azalea's "Fancy," which was climbing the charts. Given our track record with turning hip-hop into jazz, I was fully on board. I recorded a piano demo of a 1920s jazz interpretation of the instrumental and had Ashley come up with a melody to fit the rap lyrics. A bit of tinkering and—voilà!—we had something catchy and fun.

I'm so fancy
You already know
I'm in the fast lane
From LA to Tokyo...

The theme of the song worked nicely in our rearrangement in part because the decadence described in the lyrics to "Fancy" could be applied just as easily to the hedonism of the 1920s jazz scene. To really drive this point home, Ashley put together a full 1920s flapper outfit, right down to the jewelry and the fringe.

Although featuring Ashley's singing and dancing ability in the same video posed a problem for our stationary microphone, we did work in a little tap dancing for her at the high point of the arrangement for "Fancy." Immediately following her soaring vocals in the bridge, she launched into a variation of the shim-sham step that fit the vibe seamlessly. And then, right when "Fancy" became the number-one song in America, we released our version—a *tour de force* performance of outstanding vocals, rhythmic precision, and a perfectly timed dance break that quickly racked up hundreds of thousands of views.

"Fancy" contained all the elements that make a Postmodern Jukebox video so uniquely great: a strong performance, a clever arrangement twist that manipulates the context of the lyrics, and just a hint of playful irony. Iggy Azalea may have been maligned by some critics, but by no means was this a biting parody; we were simply taking the source material of the original and altering it to imagine how it would have sounded in a different historical period. In doing so, we drew parallels between the popular music of today and the music of the 1920s, as if to say that, when all's said and done, not much has changed; there will always be songs about dancing, reveling in the night, and, well...looking *fancy*.

As my subscriber base grew, I continued to expand the Dream Factory's stable of singers even more. Miche Braden, the very singer who had inspired me to become a producer in the first place, made her debut on a New Orleans blues–style remake of the Guns n' Roses song "Sweet Child o' Mine." In studying the lyrics, it had occurred to me that the '80s classic fit the popular verse/refrain format of early folk and blues songs. That Miche's Bessie Smith–like voice realizes this so stunningly and with such power on the track makes this video one of my all-time favorites.

Another superstar vocalist joined the Postmodern Jukebox universe when Broadway star Morgan James recorded a soulful, Donny Hathaway–influenced version of Maroon 5's "Maps" with us. Morgan already had a record deal, but her label wasn't quite sure what to do with her since she kind of defied classification. She had the vocal chops of Céline Dion with the blues sensibility of Nina Simone, and from the first time she sang with Postmodern Jukebox, it was obvious that she was born to perform on stages worldwide. "Maps" was a vocal master class, a soulful demonstration of the wonders of a vocal instrument trained to perfection.

The biggest viral smash of the Dream Factory that year, however, existed thanks to Kate Davis, an incredibly talented young vocalist and bassist I'd met when she auditioned for *Sleep No More*. Dressed in a patterned vintage frock, she was quiet and thoughtful, and her simple, beautiful rendition of the standard "If I Had You" left me speechless. She sang with the honesty of Billie Holiday, accompanying herself with only an upright bass. In the middle, she took a break from singing to play a yearning, lyrical bass solo. It was a masterful performance, one that showed a maturity and introspection well beyond her years.

I had been searching high and low for just the right song to showcase her remarkable talents when, seemingly out of nowhere, it materialized: Meghan Trainor's anthemic hit "All About That Bass," which was climbing the Billboard charts at the time.

The song's title was a clever analogy celebrating body positivity, but in our video, the title took on a very literal meaning, with Kate meticulously plucking out the bass notes while singing the titular refrain:

I'm all about that bass, 'bout that bass, no treble...

I entered on piano with drummer Dave Tedeschi, and the song took on a second-line, New Orleans vibe. Kate's crystal-clear voice coyly caressed the melody, and then, in the final third, she played a blazing-fast double-time upright bass solo that would make the jaw of even the most cynical redditor fall agape. When she finished, she just sort of smiled and blushed with satisfaction, and the Internet fell in love. In the weeks that followed, Kate gained tens of thousands of fans and was offered record deals left and right.

Facing a surplus of creative hunger, I went on to launch a new humorous YouTube series, titled *Saturday Morning Slow Jams*, to complement the Postmodern Jukebox series. The idea was to recast popular animated TV show themes as '90s R&B, using all the hallmarks of that style. For example, I cast my old Walmart orchestra-turned A Motown Tribute to Nickelback sideman Steve Ujfalussy in an open shirt, shades, and a gold chain as the oversexed EWI (short for "electronic wind instrument") player Steve Sweat. Our first *Slow Jam* featured the hilariously gifted Karen Marie as a character she created named POW!GRL, a counterpart to Steve Sweat that satirized the "tough girl" image of many of the female rappers in the '90s. Her take on the *DuckTales* theme was an instant hit with many memorable moments, not least at the end, when she engaged in an improvised and very sensual "duck, duck, goose" chant with Steve Sweat.

Suffice it to say that life at the Dream Factory was never dull, frequently hilarious, and sometimes almost unbelievable.

THE POWER
OF ABSURDITY

I t was the week before Halloween in 2014 when the front desk of my apartment building called to tell me that a very large clown was downstairs, holding a sign with my name on it. I wasn't concerned, which was probably a great relief for them. Personally, I find it hard to imagine there are many people a desk clerk might encounter who would be more unsettling than a giant, silent, bald-headed, sad clown with a golden crown, an old, beat-up suitcase, and a lantern.

"That's Puddles. Just send him up," I said, nonchalantly.

I had first encountered Puddles when I was working at *Sleep No More* and he was the after-show entertainment. One day I'd been informed I was to accompany him on piano—and that's all I was told.

Puddles was one part Andy Kaufman, one part Tom Jones. He started his set by stumbling through the crowd, using his lantern to light the way to the stage before literally crawling onto it. He was huge, nearly seven feet tall from the tip of his crown to the toes of his oversized shoes. Every pair of eyes in the place was on him as he dusted himself off and got behind the microphone, and then he did something brilliant: He stood there silently for

134

nearly five minutes, nervously scanning the room and pretending he was trying to motivate himself to sing. The dramatic tension was unbelievable. When Puddles *did* finally sing, he unleashed a glorious baritone that filled the room, eliciting cheers from everyone. I had never seen anything like it.

The set consisted of three songs, whose sheet music he presented to me in the form of crumpled pieces of paper fished out from his pocket. Throughout the performance he pulled various stereotypical clown props out of his suitcase, but he didn't do any magic with them. Rather, he just used them to antagonize the band, at one point sticking a long plastic flower into the face of the saxophone player while he was trying to solo. On "Lonely Guy," his grand finale, he threw tissues at the audience as he sang, ending on a big high note that resonated through the room. Then, as the audience went wild, he grabbed his suitcase and stormed off. It was perhaps the most entertaining fifteen-minute show I had ever witnessed. The ridiculousness of his act—paired with his utterly straight-faced delivery—was mesmerizing. He'd created an entire world around this character, and the more absurd his world grew, the more it drew in the audience.

The real person behind the clown was Mike Geier, or Big Mike to his friends: an eternally friendly guy who in many ways was completely the opposite of his stage persona. As he sat backstage, wiping the makeup off his face after one of our *Sleep No More* shows, I approached and told him about my YouTube channel. As a veteran musician who had learned (as had I) the value of always keeping an eye out for new opportunities, he was intrigued.

Eager to lock in his participation before he could give it more thought and potentially change his mind, I made a bold promise to him, declaring, "I know how to make Puddles into an Internet star." If Big Mike doubted me for even a split second, he didn't let it show, and we agreed to meet the next time he traveled to New

York City. The song I'd picked to arrange for his debut was "Royals" by New Zealand singer/songwriter Lorde. It seemed almost *too* perfect: a middle-aged sad clown, wearing a lopsided gold crown on his bald head, singing a song about being an outsider and disdaining the conspicuous consumption of the "royals."

Since Robyn and Cristina were both approximately the same height, I placed them on either side of Puddles and instructed them to mostly just solemnly snap their fingers throughout the duration of the video. The height difference was a visual gag, but it was also to show just how big Puddles actually was, which elevated the already absurd absurdity of the scene. Puddles' walk-on entrance was probably the most challenging part to land. His hurried exit, on the other hand, was a no-brainer: Puddles is a clown with places to be.

All we needed to do now was to get this video into the right hands and watch it spread from there. Releasing the video on Halloween, I billed Puddles as the "Sad Clown with the Golden Voice" and once again targeted the Reddit community, knowing how receptive it was to all things weird. From there, the video ripped across the Internet like wildfire. News blogs soon were picking it up left and right because of the Halloween/Stephen King connection. YouTube itself promoted the video as an example of a creative and unexpected cover. The view count soared, and Puddles became famous overnight.

In some ways, Puddles was made for the modern Internet age. He's a reflection of our loneliness and confusion in a world that's come to be increasingly characterized by those emotions. Humans have never before lived in a time of such constant stimulus and abundance of choice, and part of me wonders if experiencing life as one big dopamine rush isn't making us *less* happy instead of more so. In the end, aren't we all just wandering through life with a suitcase and a lantern, searching for a place where we belong?

TAKING THE PLUNGE

The window is open *now*. We need to jump while we can. Otherwise, we *die*."

I frowned, perplexed, and uncertain what Jaron was getting at on the other end of the phone. He did have a flair for the dramatic.

"That sounds serious," I said. "What are we talking about, again?"

Postmodern Jukebox was growing steadily in popularity, and I was enjoying the freedom of producing music from my home, with guest performers and friends constantly dropping by. Jaron, however, saw the signs that this could not last indefinitely. You-Tube audiences are fickle, and he had seen too many artists sky-rocket in popularity on the platform before falling even faster into obscurity. Crossing over into the "real world" was some-thing that needed to happen soon if we wanted to create some-thing enduring for years to come. That meant touring—and lots of it. It's difficult to make the jump from online to IRL ("in real life"), and at that point, only a few YouTube acts, like Lindsey Stirling and Boyce Avenue, had done it successfully.

The Internet, I was learning, is a place for growth, a medium where anyone with the right idea, some talent, and a lot of ambition can go from anonymous to beloved almost instantly. Indeed, it's often the best place to launch your idea and pull in potential fans. However, the fact that it's a medium on which free content is broadcast around the clock means that it's also a place where the advantage of being an established incumbent is minimal. Put simply, everyone likes the shiny new toys.

"We've got to make the jump from YouTube to the stage now, while we have the chance," Jaron continued, dramatically. "Once you have the attention on you, the meter is running. And once that window closes, it doesn't open back up." Using no fewer than three analogies to explain the situation could only mean one thing: My salad days—that time when youth, enthusiasm, and idealism all combine into one exhilarating and unstoppable force—were officially over. The salad days don't last forever, and neither does Internet fame. Quite simply, there are a host of new, exciting creative exploits happening all over the world at any given second, and the novelty of "the hot new thing" is doomed to wear off eventually. When that happens, there are only two paths forward: to give up or grow up.

Let the growing pains *commence.*

Paradoxically, the biggest hurdle we faced in moving our operation offline was convincing others that we were a legitimate act. There were a number of obstacles in that regard. One was the rotating cast; after expanding the group to incorporate a number of vocalists, it was even less clear to outsiders who was actually in our group and who was a special guest. The name was a problem, too: Scott Bradlee & Postmodern Jukebox sounded like a double bill. Even the living room setting came under scrutiny. "Why don't you have a real music video backdrop?" asked one promoter.

These were all understandable points of confusion, and it didn't help our cause that, on top of all that, YouTube acts had a reputation for not drawing many real-life fans to shows. We had been working as live performers for many years, but we were outsiders in the touring circuit, with no track record or proof of concept. The promoters would need to experience us live to appreciate what it was we were pioneering.

Fortunately, that crucial opportunity to prove ourselves materialized when YouTube invited us to perform alongside John Legend, Lindsey Stirling, and other notable acts at *YouTube OnStage Live at the Kennedy Center*. It was the break we so badly needed: a four-minute medley of Postmodern Jukebox remakes performed by our cast in front of a live audience, on a stage with full production quality and no expense spared.

In addition to Robyn, Cristina, Ashley, and Drue, we also recruited a young singer I'd recently begun working with: Kiah Victoria, a twenty-year-old NYU student with an uncommonly rich and powerful alto voice. The producers of *YouTube OnStage* went wild for her, and so we selected her to kick off our performance with a stripped-down piano-and-vocal version of Macklemore's "Same Love." From there, I arranged a medley of some of the biggest current pop hits for us to funnel through various genres. Naturally, we lined up Tim's Tambourine Guy character for the finale, though, come sound check, it became apparent that the producers didn't share our enthusiasm for him:

SHOW PRODUCER: (pointing to Tim) Can we have you in the area to the left of the piano?

TIM: Okay...but there are no lights on that part of the stage.

SHOW PRODUCER: Yes, I know.

TIM: So you're sure that's where you want me?

SHOW PRODUCER: Yes.

Playing on *Good Morning America* was a surreal experience, but it still felt like performing to a camera, so not all that different from what we did in my living room. *YouTube OnStage* was a whole other story, and when we arrived for the first rehearsal, we all just kind of stood there, looking around with dumbfounded expressions on our faces and mouths agape. The theatre was cavernous, with lights and speaker columns and state-of-the-art projectors creating vast, ever-changing visuals behind us. We were nervous, but it helped that a few of us had family members coming to the show. At least with them there, we could perhaps try to pretend it was just a student recital instead of a four-minute make-or-break, once-in-a-lifetime dream gig.

I remember looking out at four thousand people and hoping for the best, and then it all just kind of *happened*. Within an hour, the video was posted to YouTube, and we had the best sales pitch for a Postmodern Jukebox concert we could have asked for: a four-minute sample of our show, recorded live at the prestigious Kennedy Center.

We spent the rest of the night watching the other performances and hanging out at the reception with our families, most of whom were meeting each other for the first time. At one point, my mom cornered Jaron with a series of logistical questions about the recently discussed plan to send us on tour, starting with "Will there be someone there to make sure everyone gets enough sleep and is eating well?"

Once a mom, always a mom.

After circulating footage from the night's performance, ICM was able to secure us exactly what we were hoping for: a brief North America tour in small venues across the Northeast. We were taking this show on the road…whatever "this show" *was*.

In all seriousness, though, I'd had a working idea for the format of a Postmodern Jukebox stage show since long before I had the name "Postmodern Jukebox." Indeed, ever since my early ragtime piano experiments, I had viewed these pop culture transformations as existing in something of an alternate universe, with conventions as different from our world as those in comic books. The best way to present this alternate universe, I determined, would be by modeling it after variety shows from eras past, complete with an emcee, an assortment of acts, a house band—the works. My grandmother and I used to watch *The Lawrence Welk Show* together when I was young, and I described to ICM what I had in mind for the act as being "Lawrence Welk with a hundred percent more twerking." With this in mind, we were going to need more than the usual four or five members that most touring bands brought. Adding extra talent would mean stretching our already low performance fees even further, but it wasn't even a question to me; Postmodern Jukebox was an extravaganza, a spectacle, and we weren't going to give audiences anything less than the full experience right out of the gate.

I remember the day of our first appearance so vividly. We walked around Toronto, looking for any and every opportunity to tell people we were on tour. At the time, it just seemed terribly far-fetched to me that a few hundred people in a different country altogether would come out for an act whose popularity was primarily confined to YouTube, and I was secretly concerned that we'd be playing to a nonexistent crowd. This being Canada, I wondered if perhaps the Motown Nickelback show would have been a better choice.

But this was no time for calling audibles. Clad in a white dinner jacket and black bowtie, Drue was the first of our group to step out on stage. From backstage, I heard the crowd roar, and I breathed a sigh of relief.

"Hello, Toronto! My name is Drue Davis, and I will be your emcee this evening—hence the fancy suit. I picked this out myself, thank you very much. Tonight, we're going to be taking a trip back in time...."

Once he'd given his welcome speech, I joined Drue onstage to the tune of the band playing "The Final Countdown." The place was packed, I was shocked to see, and it took a moment for it to sink in. I waved awkwardly and then launched into a ragtime version of the *Super Mario Bros.* theme, an homage to my YouTube channel's roots. Next, Drue introduced Robyn, who kicked off the first full song of the night: "Thrift Shop." The audience went absolutely berserk, with people swing dancing and singing along. We knew our act was entertaining and that we could impress any old crowd that stumbled across us at a party, but to see that we had exuberant fans—and lots of them—as far away as Toronto was a real "pinch-me" moment for all of us. It rendered us speechless, as we shot incredulous glances at one another onstage. Perhaps the oddest yet most fitting validation of our fans' adoration was how dolled up they got to attend our show. Zoot suits, vintage dresses, flapper costumes—you name it, and it was there, despite the fact that I'd never mentioned anything about dressing up in our promos. It dawned on me then that, although we were just meeting them for the first time, our fans had been there on the other side of the screen all along. Like us, they had been waiting for this day to arrive.

There's one drawback to IRL performance, we soon discovered, and it's that some aspects of the production will always elude your control. Never was that more glaring than at our show in Pawtucket, Rhode Island. The night began with management at the venue unilaterally deciding to hold us for an extra hour before starting, in the hopes of selling more tickets. It was the least attended show on the run, and oddly, the fans were trending far younger than our audiences tended to be. The crowd grew understandably more restless as the delay ticked on, and they were vocal about wanting us to start. By the time we took the stage, they'd been drinking heavily for a good while, and I'd received a few angry tweets from audience members who'd grown feistily impatient or intoxicated (or both).

When we finally came onto the stage—really more of a slightly raised platform—the crowd, which had been going wild off and on, went wild once again, except this time in a somewhat menacing way. Drue was constantly interrupted by people shouting out beer-slurred requests, some for songs we'd never even covered. A couple frat brothers had taken up the refrain "Where's the clown? Bring out the clown!" as though Puddles were being kept in a cage backstage and poked with a stick until the time came to release him for his performance.

The evening hit its high point when a girl who appeared to be on drugs climbed up onstage and latched on to Drue's leg, refusing to budge. The lax security crew was of little help on this one, and so we just kind of accepted that we had to continue the show with an overzealous audience member clinging to one of our performers. If it sounds like the show was utter and complete chaos, that's because it was. We will always remember Pawtucket as the closest thing to a punk rock show that we ever played.

Our team scored a notable addition on the New Haven stop of the tour, when my old Hartford college buddy Rook came to see the show. Of all my credit-delinquent housemates, Rook—or Matt Telford, as he's legally known—was the wildcard in the bunch. He was one of the most infamous characters at the University of Hartford, despite having only studied there for a semester before failing out. He had a zany sense of humor and zero inhibitions, and he could usually be found spearheading efforts to get our household kicked out of various establishments by ridiculous means. (Fake mustaches and other "disguises" often factored into the equation.)

What else to say about Rook? Well, he certainly mastered the art of beating the system, in every sense of the word. Once, he went ten months out of a year without any employment, living entirely off the exploitation of a flaw in the promotional coupons from the Big Y grocery chain and bringing dates to Bob's Discount Furniture to take advantage of the free coffee and mini golf. No stranger to my YouTube channel, he actually starred as Rappin' Einstein in the second Postmodern Jukebox video, which was a rather bizarre, Special Theory of Relativity–inspired parody of Ke$ha's "Tik Tok" that ended abruptly after he became high on paint fumes from having to constantly reapply gray spray paint to his Einstein-ian wig/fake moustache combo. After this somewhat inauspicious debut, he'd moved out to Colorado to open a restaurant, and we lost touch for several years—though he did reappear briefly for one of the *Saturday Morning Slow Jams* videos, in which he performed a spirited and rather controversial rap about the television series *My Little Pony*.

Rook may have come to our New Haven show with the sole intention of watching, but I had other plans for him. We'd been having difficulty selling merch on the tour so far, which I'd a hunch had something to do with our CDs and posters being displayed only halfheartedly by the unenthused venue staff. Knowing that Rook's lack of inhibition could be extremely useful in the right situation, and knowing, too, that his exhibitionist tendencies were sure to attract attention, I asked if he would consider helping to sell merch for us in his own creative way. He agreed, and within minutes, he'd transformed the merch booth into a veritable bazaar of activity and energy. At one point, he got so caught up in the zeal of selling that he sold some of his own personal items:

"Hey, New Haven, have some new pants—because I'm selling mine! Everything must go!"

Tambourine Guy notwithstanding, Rook's was probably the most surprising performance of the night. In the span of a single evening, he succeeded in quadrupling the *total* amount of merch we'd sold on tour thus far. I had an idea.

"Hey Rook, do you have anything going on for the next week? There's an extra seat in the van. Can I hire you as our merch guy?"

"Yup, cool," he said, without hesitation.

"Awesome!" I thought for a second. "Do you need to go by your apartment and get some clothes or anything?"

"Nah, I'm good. I just need to buy some new pants, 'cause I sold mine."

It was settled.

I didn't have even an inkling at the time that Rook, in accepting my invitation to join our circus, was actually leaving his entire life—which included a well-paying job as a restaurant consultant and, as we later learned, a live-in girlfriend—behind. I don't think Rook had any inkling of it, either. What I'd proposed had sounded like a great adventure, something Rook was never one to turn down. It was, in the moment, as simple as that.

Not everyone was as enthused as I was by the new addition, though.

"Do you really think this is a good idea?" Adam deadpanned to me, upon hearing the news. It was more of a statement than a question. "Things are just taking off, and Rook is...well, *Rook*."

Adam was still a bit traumatized from his last encounter with Rook. Remember how I mentioned that I occasionally hired Adam to play nonpaying gigs with me and a friend in a giant koala costume? Yup, that friend was Rook. I shrugged it off.

"It's just for a few shows. Besides, you *have* to admit he's creative."

Even Adam couldn't dispute that. "Okay," he said, resignedly, "but if he tackles me in a bear suit again, I'm out."

As our tour progressed, demand for us grew. Second shows were added in New York and DC to accommodate eager audiences, and promoters from cities not originally on our tour were now requesting dates. Jaron was convinced that if we wanted to make it happen, leaping to the next level of international act wasn't out of the question. After all, we were already scheduled to play a high-profile wedding in Monaco a few weeks after the U.S. run ended; if we used the profits from it to secure a bus, we could easily pull off a month-long European tour and take a stab at establishing ourselves overseas.

I, however, was skeptical. The upfront costs of the U.S. run were hard enough for me to absorb.

"I don't know, Jaron. . . . I was really looking forward to actually making money on a gig."

"What do you do when you're at the casino and you win big?"

"Um. Walk away?"

"NO!" he replied, emphatically. "You DOUBLE DOWN! You take that chance to win! *Even bigger!*"

Did Jaron's strategy sound like a surefire way to leave the casino without the clothes on our backs? Absolutely. But his excitement was contagious, and the prospect of touring Europe seemed worth the risk of possibly coming back with emptied pockets (or without pockets, period). I decided to double down and made a mental note to ask Rook how to get the maximum price when selling one's pants—just in case things went south.

I had still never traveled outside North America, and I was psyched to see Europe. The rest of the cast greeted the news happily, for the most part. Adam, who loved traveling, was probably the most excited of us all, followed closely by Cristina, who manically rattled off every cuisine she planned on eating, before dashing off to purchase several pairs of "Gatti pants"—what were essentially just elastic-waist pajama pants—as her travel attire. Robyn expressed enthusiasm, too, though with slight hesitation; some things about touring—from the lack of decent showers and cramped dressing rooms to the confusing sound checks that frequently ended in tears and pressure-filled onstage environments—were proving to be challenging for her.

"How about we go to Europe and *not* play shows?" she said, only half-joking.

Off we flew to Manchester, where we set our sights on what would become our very first tour bus—a used, bright yellow number with its rental company's name stenciled on the side in Comic Sans. The font alone should have tipped us off to the fact that we were in for a bumpy ride, but we were too blinded by the thrill of being, suddenly, a band that traveled by tour bus to notice. As it turned out, this bus of ours was equipped with some really questionable amenities, which included, but were not limited to, the following: a broken door that swung open at inopportune times, such as while the bus was on the highway or rounding a tight curve; a sink whose water went from freezing cold to scalding hot in a matter of seconds; and a lookout hatch on the ceiling of the upper level, which would have been lovely, save for the fact that Europe is notorious for its dangerously low clearance tunnels. To cap it off, the whole vehicle had a musty scent to it, similar to that of a wall-to-wall carpeted basement that hadn't been aired out since the '70s. After I sent him pictures, Jaron, ever the reliable optimist where Postmodern Jukebox was concerned, called the bus "vibey."

To ensure that our first tour overseas went smoothly while he was in LA making deals, Jaron sent along one of his associates, Jordan Howard, to assist with tour management duties. An ardent music fan and devoted roadie, Jordan had been managing

147

YouTube acts since the days when the YouTube music scene was just taking off. He met Jaron while working in Nashville and soon found himself working side-by-side with him, often by playing the role of "good cop" in meetings with Jaron's clients and business partners. Indeed, they made for a balanced management team. Where Jaron could be analytical and aggressive in dealings, Jordan was personable and friendly. His people skills proved a tremendous asset with us abroad, getting promoters to better some of the smaller venues' less-than-stellar conditions and helping to keep the peace among the cast.

Over the course of the European tour, our shows became increasingly polished, allowing each performer's star qualities to shine. One of my favorite memories from the trip took place in Prague, where we performed to a sold-out venue of eight hundred dancing fans who called us back for not one but two encores—the latter of which turned into me playing and singing an impromptu cover of "Dream" by The Everly Brothers. For someone who, only a year before, had only ever been treated at gigs as the background music, being the main event at last truly felt like a dream.

There was no question about it: No longer just a salad days side project, Postmodern Jukebox had evolved into something of far greater magnitude—something deserving of the entirety of my attention and creativity every day. At last, I had achieved artistic freedom.

HOW GETTING KICKED OUT LANDED US ON HOLLYWOOD'S MAP

Hi Scott:
I have received complaints that you have musicians come to your apartment on a regular basis to rehearse live music in your apartment. Please keep in mind that it is a violation of your lease to make undue noise that can be heard outside of your unit. Although I am a music lover myself I am sure you can understand that some residents prefer not to hear your music. Please contact me with any questions.

Thanks for your cooperation.

I can't say this letter from the property manager of the building that housed the Dream Factory was entirely unexpected. After all, what I rented from them was very much a seven-hundred-square-foot one-bedroom apartment, surrounded on all sides by other seven-hundred-square-foot one-bedroom apartments. It was a reasonable request. Call me stubborn, call me cocky (the success was starting to go to my head...just a little bit), but I wasn't ready to relinquish my salad days. And so, I made a conscious decision to carry on as I'd been carrying on all along, complaints be damned.

This worked until it didn't, when I was brusquely kicked out—just as I had been from my Hartford rental a decade earlier. The straw that broke the camel's back? A zealous, noisy tap dancing cover of a Jason Derulo song. I was nearing thirty-three and again without a home; on the upside, however, my new displacement had the effect of freeing me up from the mind-set that I *had* to live in this city. I could do my job from anywhere!

Living in Los Angeles had never really appealed to me. There was a certain rawness to my artistic methods and to those of my collaborators that was quintessentially East Coast, and on top of that, I couldn't imagine being so far away from my friends and family. Yet the timing of my eviction lined up precisely with an opportunity to play a three-month weekly residency at one of Hollywood's hottest nightclubs, Hyde Sunset.

As usual, Jaron's reaction was one of extreme excitement. "Dude, imagine doing a Postmodern Jukebox show and Leonardo DiCaprio and Rihanna are watching it, and Rihanna's like, I want to sing with you, and Leo's got all these models and they're taking pictures, and Gary Busey's acting all crazy and shit, and *TMZ* rolls up, asking 'Who's *this hot new act that's taking LA by storm?*'"

All right, yes, that did sound strangely fun. I pictured Rihanna as a flapper, Leo as a mobster, and Gary Busey perched beside a nearby bathtub, making gin.

The goal, as Jaron explained to me, was to use this residency as a way to get in front of some of Hollywood's biggest players, who tended not to frequent shows alongside the general public but were known to enjoy the club scene. At Hyde, we'd be bringing Postmodern Jukebox to *them*, in a creative, immersive way. Furthermore, the hot spot could function as an incubator for new ideas, since we'd be developing a whole new show tailored to the space. I loved the idea of taking an environment that wasn't intended for live music and turning it into a home for the ever-changing Postmodern Jukebox. I ran the opportunity by our featured performers at the time, and it was met with resounding approval. PMJ—the acronym for the group that had caught on among our fans—was westward bound.

To raise funds for the move, we announced back-to-back mini tours—appropriately dubbed the "Eviction Tour"—up and down the East and West Coasts. Our plan was to play Hyde every Wednesday and hit the road on tour in between. It made for a packed schedule, but playing Hyde so regularly would give us a nice home base. Worst-case scenario, if it all fell to crap, we'd come back to New York in three months' time, sunkissed and perhaps waxing poetic about the joys of kale. I rented a large house in the San Fernando valley town of Van Nuys for the eight of us making the move. I'd yet to see the place, but Jaron assured me that he had checked it out and that it "had a vibe." This made me immediately suspicious.

Indeed, it did have a vibe—one that screamed either "reality TV house" or "porn set," depending on your viewing habits. Each bedroom was wired with cameras that fed into what could only be called a control room. The interior was '70s groovy, with red shag carpeting throughout and, in the master bedroom, a plush red bed straight out of a Mount Airy Lodge commercial. I wouldn't want to take a black light to the place, but all in all, it was in good shape and would meet our needs just fine. We celebrated that first night by drinking champagne in the hot tub (until the motor unexpectedly gave out, at which point it turned into a lukewarm tub).

Although the rent itself was fairly reasonable, actually

providing for eight people was beyond my financial capabilities at the time. The upfront costs of concurrently moving and prepping for tour—flights, rent, food, basic furniture, audio backline, shipping, plus two tour buses and tour salaries—amounted to much more than I'd anticipated paying. Keeping up with expenses became even more difficult when our Hyde appearance got pushed back by a month and a few other gigs fell through. Suddenly, we found ourselves on what appeared to be a two-week vacation in Van Nuys with no income.

It didn't help matters that I could only afford to rent two cars for the eight of us, leading to a prevailing sense of being under house arrest for a few in our group. No one had any outside means of making money, so the simple act of taking a taxi downtown to shake off the stir-crazy was largely out of the question. Our tour manager, usually so dependable as a calming force in the face of chaos, looked to be on the verge of snapping.

When our Hyde show did finally launch, it was fraught with problems. The sound system was meant for DJs, not bands, and it turned into a nightmare of feedback when we introduced our sixteen-mic setup. The immersive speakeasy setting that I had pictured—replete with dancing flappers and assorted pop-up performances throughout the room—required more floor space than was at our disposal. "Immersive," in this case, meant having a dancer knock a drink into your lap. There was no stage lighting to illuminate the performers, and Rook's makeshift lighting rig, consisting of gaffe tape and a broom handle suspended from the ceiling, was met with horror by the club's management. It wasn't *all* bad, though; lots of fans flocked in to see and meet us on opening night, and none other than Puddles even dropped by to sing a few songs. The sight of him tossing crumbled Kleenex at a bored, snobbish couple seated in the front row gave us all a much-needed laugh.

We worked out the kinks, eventually, and once we did, our Wednesdays at Hyde became the incubator for new talent that I'd wanted it to be—my latest laboratory. Broadway legend Shoshana Bean sang with us as a special guest one night early on in our residency, and she wasted no time introducing us to her address book of LA talent. In addition to being one of the most amazing vocalists in the world, Shoshana was also a supremely warm, generous, and enthusiastic soul—a rarity in any industry but especially in ours. Many future PMJ stars made their debuts with the group in Hyde's intimate setting, where the prevailing mood was that of a jam session at a party; nothing was really rehearsed, and sometimes we had performances that veered off the rails. But then there were those moments of inspiration—like catching lightning in a bottle—that made it all worthwhile.

I began working with two other vocalists who would become repeat collaborators in the future: Von Smith and Ariana Savalas. I learned about Von Smith in the most twenty-first-century way possible: through a cover of *our* cover of "Thrift Shop" that he tweeted to me. On first watch, I was amazed at how this singer, who looked to be in his early twenties, had completely harnessed his voice in a way that allowed him to sing complicated phrases and extremely high notes with laser sharp precision and breath control.

Von grew up as a small-town kid in Kansas, idolizing the great Broadway, jazz, and soul singers of the past. When a live video of him performing "And I Am Telling You" went viral and led to an appearance on *Ellen*, he'd experienced his own tale of YouTube success. Later, he competed on *American Idol* and scored a slot opening for Lady Gaga in Brisbane by winning the reality show *Opening Act*. After a lot of time spent in the spotlight, Von was newly trying to take some space from mainstream media and embark on a journey of finding his own voice as an artist. Despite all his gifts, he was humble to a fault and concerned that his performance wasn't PMJ-worthy. That he was stricken with the same perfectionism I had battled for years was obvious, and I felt for him.

Ariana Savalas. It was a name I'd been hearing quite a bit that year, 2014. The youngest daughter of legendary actor and *Kojak* star Telly Savalas, Ariana was making waves as a jazz singer in Los Angeles and had mentioned her love for Postmodern Jukebox onstage at a few of her club dates. She was a friend of both Kai and Jaron, and when we eventually connected, I was pleasantly surprised to find that she had a larger-than-life personality to go with her rich alto voice. Despite having grown up in a show business family, she'd elected to go to Catholic school, with the intention of becoming a nun. That was before the allure of per-forming propelled her into a colorful career that included a brief stint as a pop star in Greece. Self-described as "Miss Piggy meets Peggy Lee," she favored an eccentric wardrobe of leopard- and cheetah-print pants, large sunglasses, and fur coats. The first time she sang with us, it was at a party hosted by *Full House* producer Jeff Franklin, at his Beverly Hills home. Somewhere in the middle of "No Diggity"—the song we had selected as her PMJ debut—Ariana ventured out into the audience, ad-libbing innuendos and sitting on the laps of the older gentlemen in atten-dance. Her comedic timing was flawless; she was a machine gun of one-liners and quick gags, like holding the microphone out to her victim and asking, "What's your name?" and then abruptly yanking it back, before they even had a chance to answer, and intensely intoning, "I don't care." We had a new character in our universe, completely unlike ingenues Robyn, Cristina, and Ashley: the vixen.

In some ways, being forced to move across the country was exactly the shake-up we needed to build out our talent base.

A word to the wise: If ever you should feel like you have *too much* choice in life, remember that life still makes a good deal of choices for you. You can only play with the hand you've been dealt, and options that you have in one moment often disappear the next if you don't make moves to capitalize on them. The beauty in this is that drastic change is the catalyst for personal growth, and personal growth is a vital component of the artist's life, with each phase of it bringing new challenges, new opportunities, and a new perspective.

Those initial months in Los Angeles had set my career on an upward trajectory. The influx of new performers sated my creative hunger, and in between recording and performing, I was taking meetings from labels, television producers, and other potential partners. Not only was awareness of the band on the rise but being fresh to Los Angeles made me something of a novelty, which helped create some healthy competition between potential partners. We even performed at an awards show, our first: the Internet-based Streamy Awards. Jaron smuggled a trophy belonging to rapper Pitbull out of the Beverly Hilton for us, at the behest of no one, and so while we didn't technically win an award, we walked away from the night feeling like stars.

Then everything fell apart.

THINGS FALL APART

I stood surveying the scene, then turned to Rook.

"Hmm... maybe it'll look better if we turn the fire on?"

"You don't want to do that; it's full of rat poison," he said matter-of-factly.

"Rat poison?"

"Yeah, I got covered in it climbing out in my Santa costume for the video shoot. Now everything tastes like metal."

We stared at the fireplace for some time, silent. "Let's just hang some stockings off of the piano and film this stupid thing," I said finally.

It was November 2014, and we were under the gun trying to deliver the Christmas album, *A Very Postmodern Christmas*, that we'd promised our fans. It hadn't been going well. In fact, we'd just learned earlier in the day that the song we recorded the previous night had to be scrapped because we'd placed the microphones facing the wrong direction. To be precise, *Rook* had placed the microphones facing the wrong direction, but he was working so hard to keep everything from falling apart that I couldn't bring myself to tell him it was his fault.

We tried our hardest to transform our porn-set household into a quaint Christmas village, but the holiday spirit remained largely absent. We had just wrapped what turned out to be the semi-disastrous "Eviction Tour," whose nadir was reached during a pre-show dinner argument that left half the cast in tears and our tour manager going to sleep on the bus instead of mixing the sound for our show. Now, back in LA, people weren't speaking to one another, and the house arrest situation was feeling more and more like incarceration in an actual prison. Robyn, Ashley, and Cristina had been the featured vocalists on our tour and at Hyde, but the recent influx of new talent signaled that this was to be even more of a rotating cast in the future. That didn't feel particularly good for three singers who had uprooted their lives in New York to come work with us in LA, and they weren't the only ones who were unhappy; others in the house were growing resentful of the house arrest situation, too. While I was off taking meetings with industry people, they were stuck in Van Nuys, wondering why they were even there. The promises of career advancement and networking opportunities were coming true— but mostly just for me.

My relationship with Robyn had deteriorated as well. The changing group dynamic was creating upsetting personal upheaval for her, as more established singers came into the picture and her role as the group's star vocalist diminished onstage. Postmodern Jukebox had pretty much cemented itself as my bona fide obsession offstage as well as on by now, and I was spending less and less time with Robyn, often leaving her behind at the house while I attended meetings and events. Watching me grow ever more distant pained her, and we found ourselves getting into fights after shows. In an effort to assuage the guilt, I would try to rationalize to myself that I'd given Robyn her dream career, that without me she would never have reached her true potential. Deep down, though, I knew none of it was true; I knew that she'd never asked for this life I'd foisted on her. She had simply wanted to sing because it made her happy to do so, but having to "compete" with professional singers made it all significantly less fun.

To make matters worse, ever since our relationship was exposed during Postmodern Jukebox's *Good Morning America* appearance, fans had been weighing in relentlessly on what *should* have been our private lives, often in an attempt to stir up drama between us. It wasn't unusual for Robyn to receive a fan message warning her that I looked particularly cozy in a photo with some new female singer or another. It wasn't a healthy environment for a relationship, and I think we both knew that eventually, something would have to give.

After one particularly tear-filled night, Robyn turned to me with a terrified look in her eyes.

"When will our life go back to normal?" she asked. "This isn't real life. When will we do karaoke and get breakfast at Astor Bake Shop in the morning, like regular people?"

I was silent, but I didn't need to speak; the somber look on my face said it all. There was no normal anymore, and I didn't know what to do about it.

I've yet to figure out whether it's possible to throw yourself wholeheartedly into a career as an artist or an entrepreneur without it causing your personal relationships to suffer—at least somewhat. Even before Postmodern Jukebox, I had a tendency to put my creative projects ahead of all else, which resulted in my hurting some people who truly cared for me. I would venture to guess that the work lives and relationships of many successful creative people aren't as perfectly harmonious as the media profiles suggest. Being in the public eye makes maintaining these relationships incredibly difficult, and I think to suggest otherwise is a bit disingenuous. The life of an artist (or an artist's romantic partner) isn't for everyone; it can be an isolating and lonely experience for those who have a greater need for stability.

By Christmas, our lease had ended, and with it we closed a particularly tumultuous chapter of PMJ history. There were still a lot of hurt feelings among our performers and crew members, and it wasn't clear to me if any of them wanted to be involved with the project anymore. This was especially saddening because they were more than just colleagues; they were my good friends, too. Robyn and I separated, she returning to New York and I planning to remain in LA. Postmodern Jukebox was bigger than ever, yet I ended 2014 with no attachments, no permanent place to call home, and now possibly no band. My childhood dream had come true—but at what cost?

UNCOVERING THE AWESOME POWER OF COLLABORATION

Y ou know, you can live here, if you want. We can clean up the living room, and you can record there, and I'll cook for everyone and show them all your old pictures! Doesn't that sound *fun*?"

My mom flitted about giddily as she served Christmas dinner at the New Jersey house where I grew up.

"I'm a thirty-three-year-old man, Mom," I said, defensively. "I'm not moving back home."

"I'm just *so excited* to have you back, even if it's just for a little while. You know, my friends at Zumba class told me that people in LA are all a bit wacky. Who's that guy—the one who jumped on Oprah's couch? That's the kind of person that I imagine lives there."

I just shook my head, bit my tongue, and enjoyed the home-cooked meal. I wasn't there to argue, and frankly I didn't really know how I felt about LA after the chaos of the past few months. My mind was on the major tour of Europe that was only a month away, and of my Van Nuys housemates, only three had elected to remain with the project. I was tasked with essentially rebuilding Postmodern Jukebox from scratch.

I wasn't sure how I was going to recover from losing so many key people at once. One thing was certain, though: I wasn't going to repeat the mistakes I had made in the past. This time, I wasn't going to uproot anyone's life, and I wasn't going to make anyone feel undervalued. I vowed to let go of my control-freak tendencies and embrace the possibilities of more egalitarian collaboration.

Every successful project is, at its core, a collaborative one, and Postmodern Jukebox was no exception. It would have been a huge waste not to utilize all the talent at my disposal just so that I could feel like I had done it all on my own—and that's if it ever got far enough to even warrant bragging rights. Part of leading well is being able to objectively evaluate the individual skills of your teammates and then guide them in a way that enables them to make the most significant contribution. You'll never be able to do this unless you're willing to get out of the way and give others the space to be great.

I met with Jaron in damage-control mode, looking to come up with a plan for Europe. News of Robyn's and my breakup had gotten out, and her fans were sending me angry messages. We had agreed that both of us going on the European tour right now would be disastrous in the long term, but fans felt otherwise, and they certainly weren't holding back expressing it.

"Used to like you guys. Won't be seeing you now that Robyn's gone. Good luck, you're gonna need it without her," read one angry note I got on Facebook.

"Robyn was the only reason I liked you guys. Nice job ruining PMJ you talentless looser [sic]," read another.

Jaron wasn't all that concerned.

"We're in showbiz; controversy is good! I wish you had *more* drama in your life!" he joked.

But I wasn't laughing. It was bad enough to have to go through a romantic breakup with someone I cared for; the feeling that PMJ might never recover from the musical breakup between its leader and its star performer was too much to bear.

Jaron felt that we did a disservice to everyone—fans and cast alike—by not properly defining Postmodern Jukebox as a rotating cast from the very start. The concept of a "band" is easy for people to understand, but an "experiential musical collective" is something else entirely. We were creating a new sort of entertainment, one that had potential to be long-lasting and global and to reach millions of people. If we were simply a band, we'd have two, maybe three good years, and then we'd fade away as individual members tired of the routine and quit to explore other projects and start families. It was crucial that we rebuild the Postmodern Jukebox model with clarity.

To do this, we decided to split up the personnel on our European tour, so that cast members came in and out of the tour instead of remaining on the bus for the entire two months. It was more expensive, and it was more work, but we wanted to demonstrate that the show is *still* Postmodern Jukebox, no matter who's onstage. There was no single "star"; the secret to Postmodern Jukebox's magic was that it came from an ensemble effort. Even the set list, we decided, would change to accommodate the ever-changing cast and each person's individual strengths. I loved this because it captured the spirit of jazz improvisation. Each Postmodern Jukebox show would be its own unique, ephemeral experience, never to be duplicated exactly.

The next step was to build the cast. Between the performers I'd met during our Hyde residency and the singers I recorded with at the Dream Factory, I had a lot of great choices, but I wasn't sure if we could afford them. After all, many of these singers worked constantly on television and Broadway. There wasn't much of a budget, so we would have to bank on being able to win them over by showing them how our platform could help their individual careers.

"Don't worry," Jaron said, "this is a *dream gig.* Just leave it to me; this is where I excel. I know how to talk to managers."

I winced. That was the part I was afraid of.

Calm is not a word that anyone would use to describe Jaron, but he saved the vast majority of his anger reserves for other managers. After a heated back-and-forth with one manager about who should pay for excess baggage fees, he attached an image of the dictionary definition of "look a gift horse in the mouth" to summarize his rival's request. In another contentious email exchange, he told a manager that he "didn't know shit about the music business." Jaron's temper may have been common knowledge, but his persistence was legendary, and he was able to somehow pull off acquiring every singer I had requested for the European tour while keeping it all below budget. I went from being worried about the collapse of PMJ to wildly optimistic about its future. When it came to our talent roster for this European tour, we had a veritable embarrassment of riches. In addition to previous PMJ singers like Cristina, Ariana, Kiah, and Morgan, we also had some new cast members that I was thrilled to get to work with: Mykal Kilgore, Casey Abrams, and Haley Reinhart.

Mykal Kilgore had appeared in Morgan's "Maps" video six months earlier as a backup singer, and he'd demonstrated some serious vocal chops even then. A Broadway vet, he had recently sent me an unbelievable, high-energy cover of Justin Timberlake's "Pusher Love Girl" from one of his live performances. One listen, and I was already envisioning his potential as the show's host.

Hyde saxophonist Jacob Scesney was responsible for connecting me with former *American Idol* finalist Casey Abrams. While not too familiar with his body of work, I'd been blown away by a YouTube clip I'd seen of him demonstrating a soulful voice and great jazz bass skills. On the day of the Hyde show, Casey was set to come by our afternoon sound check so that we could work out a tune to play. For whatever reason, I expected to him to be an introverted, scholarly fellow.

"Duuude, what's up, man? I'm Casey. Sweet place, man."

He gave me a big hug, and the stale aroma of marijuana filled my nostrils. *This is going to be interesting*, I thought.

Apparently, I wasn't the only one thrown off by his appearance; one of the managers at Hyde had tried to get him to leave when he first entered the venue, probably mistaking him for a homeless person. (This was a recurring theme for us; on another occasion, a different manager had reacted similarly when he found Rook, having just returned from an exhausting day of travel, lying facedown in the parking lot, taking a nap.) But as much as Casey looked the part of the spaced-out hippie, he was absolutely on his game once he got on the upright bass and began to play. He suggested the song "I'm Not the Only One" by Sam Smith, and he caught every change I played almost instantly in the way that only a true natural musician can do. His voice was strong and gruff; he combined blues sensibilities with Jack Black–style theatrics, and he tore into the upright bass with such intensity that I half expected the strings to come off the fretboard.

"Hey, you're amazing!" I told him after the show. "Would you be down to record that tune with us?"

"Dude," he said, nodding his head, "that would be *dope*."

We filmed our New Orleans–style arrangement of "I'm Not the Only One" a couple weeks later. It became a staple of PMJ's repertoire and proved to be a real crowd-pleaser on tour.

I first met Haley Reinhart in the most random of places: at Casey's Halloween party later that month. (You'd have to ask her what her costume was that year, but I'm pretty sure I was dressed as a zombie.) We weren't familiar with each other's work at the time, but I did recall several PMJ fans having already told me that she would be a great fit for the project. Apparently, she had done *Idol* a few years back and had released an album on Interscope, but she wasn't one to bring up her accomplishments; she simply told me she was "trying to be a singer/songwriter." She said she was curious about the work I was doing with PMJ, and so I invited her to sit in with us in our next show at Hyde.

It was a full house at Hyde the night that we first performed with Haley. The weekly Wednesday night crowd, which had begun as only about seventy or so fans at the start of our residency, had by now grown much larger as word spread of the old Hollywood–style shows we were doing. Haley showed up just in time for the last set, glamorously dressed in a red dress and matching hat. I asked her if she wanted to sing something, and she agreed; she already knew the lyrics to "All About That Bass."

From the moment she began singing, the crowd fell silent and collectively reached for their cell phones to record this impromptu performance. She had the glamorous look of a celebrity, true, but it was her voice that stopped everyone in their tracks. Her voice was pitch perfect, yet so colorful; she brought husky low tones and high belted notes to the song that I never would have thought to incorporate on my own. Her jazz-tinged embellishments on the melody and relaxed phrasing subtly showed that she knew the history behind what she sang, as well. Her performance ended to thunderous applause.

The Tove Lo song "Habits" was getting a lot of airplay at the time, and its wistful chorus melody reminded me of the sound of old French jazz records. I figured Haley's melodic sensibilities would be able to add a whole new dimension to the song, and we began jamming on it. I changed the chord progression to evoke the sound of tunes played by Django Reinhardt and the Hot Club of France, imagining acoustic guitar and the lonely timbre of a clarinet filling the space. Haley was on the same wavelength as me; she altered the melody to the style of Ella Fitzgerald and even added a bit of tasteful scat singing. I knew we had something great.

After a week of rehearsals, our next tour left from New York City and began with the most comfortable red-eye flight (yes, it can and does exist, but it usually requires the plane to be less than half-full), which landed us in Northern Ireland. The show there was electric, and the crowd of a few hundred people was livelier than we'd expected. Afterward, we went to a bar down the road and celebrated with drinks, dancing, and—in Casey's case—a Queen singalong on an old piano. He played and sang "Bohemian Rhapsody" at the top of his lungs, against the advice of Broadway vets Morgan and Mykal. Sure enough, Casey lost his voice and didn't get it back for the rest of the first week of shows—and learned an important lesson about vocal health.

Empowered as a team of collaborators bringing everything we had, we hit our stride over the course of the tour in a way we never had before. During "Such Great Heights," Kiah consistently got the entire audience on their feet, dancing and cheering for her. Morgan's soprano was flexible, strong, and dazzling. Night after night, she belted out the high G# in "Maps" to thunderous applause. She even worked in a brief bit of Mozart's famous "Queen of the Night" aria for a curtain call when the tour passed through Vienna.

Mykal, meanwhile, was becoming something of a superstar as emcee. Known for his roles in several Broadway musicals, he possessed a pitch-perfect high tenor honed by years of singing Gospel. He had a big personality to match his big voice and commanded attention from the instant he stepped onstage. A quick thinker, he was never at a loss for words and often came up with lots of bits and introductions for the cast. During "Roar," he finished by falling backward and continuing to sing while rolling around on the stage à la Patti LaBelle. It was electrifying.

The first half of the European run included stops at some venues decidedly larger than what we were used to playing. We wound up selling out two London venues—O2 Shepherd's Bush and O2 Indigo—which both held over two thousand people. London had emerged as the biggest city for Postmodern Jukebox worldwide, and we were recognized around town and mobbed after shows.

Even as we were maturing as a group and becoming more professional, we *did* still know how to keep it light and silly. In what had become something of a ritual, we would gather 'round during sound check each night for a pre-show show-and-tell segment called "Talent Corner," in which different cast members would be called upon to show off a non-musical prowess. The idea came from the discovery that one of our horn players had been writing sexually charged haikus during his off time. The inaugural Talent Corner featured a reading of a collection of these haikus by said horn player, in what can only be described as a kind of HR department nightmare. Other notable Talent Corner performances included a hilarious tour roast by Adam Kubota and a performance of "Take Me to Merch," Morgan James' tribute to Rook's duties as merch seller. Talent Corner reached its peak when Rook himself performed a magic-show-gone-wrong that ended abruptly with Casey on the ground, writhing in pain, after being struck in the groin during Rook's attempt to make him "disappear."

We received a warm welcome all over Europe. In Warsaw, Poland, where the audience shrieked with every subsequent cast member reveal, we witnessed a twelve-year-old girl cry tears of joy at a post-show signing session and a man pledge to tattoo all of our signatures on his arm. (I told him that this was a bad idea, for the record.)

The 2015 European tour was an enormous success. The only thing close to a calamity was a few cast members losing their luggage en route to Germany, though it didn't affect Casey, who pretty much wore the same clothes every day. Although the tour didn't net any money after accounting for all the expenses, it proved beyond a shadow of a doubt that we'd hit on something incredibly special in our revised approach to touring not as a band but as a movement. None of us fit the mold of conventional pop performers, yet there we were, getting stopped to pose for pictures and sign autographs in the streets of cities we'd never been to before. Parents told us that our group helped them bridge the generation gap and find some common ground with their kids, who in turn told us that we inspired them to take music lessons. Lovers of retro culture thanked us for making their interests "cool."

The cast's touring experience had also improved greatly, thanks to our new tour manager, Will Pepple. Although we still had long travel days and less-than-stellar dressing room conditions—some of these things are inevitable when you go from venue to venue—his attention to detail ensured that things ran as smoothly as possible, and his easygoing nature made for a calming and fun environment. Before each show, he gave the cast a mock pep talk to loosen everyone up: "So guys, listen...I think tonight's the night that we're going to get signed. I spoke to a few members of the press, and they agreed to cover the show. They write for a high school paper here in Germany, and one of them actually has a cousin that *took a picture* with David Hasselhoff. So, no pressure...but tonight could be *big*."

The entire road crew—Will, Rook, our photographer, Brave,

and our stage manager, Dylan—got a kick out of the camarade-rie that came from touring abroad, and they formed their own little clique, just as the singers and instrumentalists had done. Once their work was completed, they'd often disappear to cele-brate "Roadie Friday" (aka the night before a day off) by scour-ing whatever city we were in ahead of time to identify the very worst dive bars. Sometimes—as in the case of Rook and Brave in Christiania, the notorious self-governed district of Denmark—this resulted in a day of violent illness from ingesting drinks that had apparently been spiked.

I was especially thrilled by the tour's success since its cast was almost wholly different from that of the first European tour, and yet the show had only been met with more praise and excitement. It was gratifying to see our recently implemented, rotating collec-tive model—where everyone brought unique talents to the table—paying off. No performers were interchangeable, we'd shown, but neither were any completely indispensable. Somewhere between a band, a theatrical performance, and a Blue Man Group–like revue, Postmodern Jukebox was an entirely new format for live entertainment.

Perhaps most importantly, I was getting better at trusting the talented performers I had brought onboard. Mykal and Morgan helped tighten up the script and the transitions between perfor-mances. Adam helped run rehearsals and handle press when I was especially swamped with work. Ariana added an element of audience engagement that made each show particularly memora-ble for men in the front row over the age of sixty. I was realizing that I had some blind spots when it came to putting together a show and that that was okay. I wasn't *supposed* to do everything myself or tell people what to say or how to act. I was supposed to build a team and bring out the best in them.

Meanwhile, back home, America was excitedly tuning in

to *American Idol* to watch a young street performer from Virginia stand before the judges and give her all on a New Orleans zydeco–style version of "Fancy," performed with an accordion strapped to her chest.

The arrangement was fun and colorful, and the audience went crazy, as if her performance were the freshest, most unique take on a popular song they had heard all season. *Idol* host Ryan Seacrest eventually made his way over to the singer to ask where she'd gotten the idea for the arrangement. With millions tuned in, she raised the mic and gave her answer: "It's actually a band called Postmodern Jukebox, that takes modern-day songs and puts them in a different era....I love them, they're great."

And just like that, the name of the project I'd launched out of a basement in Astoria had made it to prime time.

TAPPING THE
AUTHENTIC SELF

I was standing in an auditorium in a foreign country, surrounded by a crowd of fans, when someone tapped me on the shoulder to request an autograph. I'd finished a show just twenty minutes prior, and I was sweaty and slightly disheveled in my suit. Rook jumped in to intercept the Sharpie being held out to me.

"Hey, guys, he's done signing for now," he said. "Scotty, we gotta get you to dinner."

That's Rook's code to allow me to exit gracefully, his rationale being that *everyone* understands the importance of not missing dinner—even at eleven o'clock at night.

"It's okay, Rook. I can sign a couple more." It's nice having a team that helps you look like the good guy in front of your fans. I smiled at the fan in front of me now, a tall fellow wearing a waistcoat and a bowtie. Then I took the poster and Sharpie and wrote SCOTT BRADLEE in all capital letters; it's the same signature I've had since fourth grade.

Also nice: to be so wholeheartedly embraced for being the person I am. I'd spent most of my life prior to the PMJ years searching for an identity—something that I could present to the world that would neatly sum up just who I, Scott Bradlee, really *was*.

Was I a jazz pianist? A music producer? A faux British New Wave front man? When I was an adolescent, I never felt comfortable in my own skin. So, I tried on different identities the way most people try on clothing. One year, I devoured classic literature and tried to present myself as a cultured intellectual. Another year, I lifted weights, wore silver chains around my neck, and tried to pass as a street-smart Jersey tough guy. Obviously, neither attempt was too successful, since my search didn't stop there.

I had always assumed that when I finally stepped into the right identity, I would just know it; I would magically become *myself*, and success and happiness would follow. I didn't want to be my actual self, you see, because I believed the thing that I had always been *truly* passionate about—so-called "vintage" music—was far too niche and weird to ever allow me to experience such success.

What I discovered in the course of launching PMJ is that we're not intrigued by people who are simply trying to play a role but rather by people who are unapologetically authentic. It was not until I finally learned to embrace myself and the things that made me *me* that I experienced any level of success.

In high school, you'll recall from earlier in my story, I—like every other outcast searching for his identity—had felt a special connection to Radiohead's "Creep." Years later, when I started composing arrangements for *Sleep No More* and met Karen Marie for the first time, she suggested we add "Creep" to the set list. I was taken aback. *How did she know how much I loved that song?* I wondered.

We reimagined the song in 6/8 time, lending it the feel of Etta James' "At Last." I even included the intro to "At Last" on piano, and Karen—ever the comedian—ended the demo by quoting a line from TLC's very different hit song also named "Creep." We recorded the Postmodern Jukebox version in August 2014, in

Astoria's Samurai Hotel Studio. It was an honest, touching version of the song, performed by a singer who—like me—had truly connected to the lyrics.

While on tour in Europe with Postmodern Jukebox, Haley Reinhart fell in love with the arrangement and asked if she could perform it live with us. We had never played this arrangement on tour before, and I was curious how it would go over, so we added it to the set list in Lyon, France. The reaction was immediate; it was the most talked-about performance of the night. In addition to Haley's raw, powerful vocals, there was something else that caused people to connect intensely with the performance: It felt authentic to us as a group. The audience could infer from the candor of our performance that the song's somber lyrics must have reflected each of our own personal experiences, and likely their own experiences, as well. We were former music kids with an unusual soft spot for the kind of music our grandparents listened to; in your typical American high school environment, none of us could have even pretended to fit in, and I think our audiences could recognize that.

Haley's take on the vocal line of "Creep" was all her own, borrowing from elements of jazz, soul, and classic rock. In many ways, it was a perfect vehicle for her artistry as a vocalist, blending all her influences together into one powerful ballad. The European audiences loved it; the one-two punch of Morgan's stark "Take Me to Church" followed by Haley's "Creep" made for an eight-minute master class on how to sing a ballad. Haley's worldwide fan base—dubbed "Haliens"—showered her and PMJ with lots of love at both the shows and the pre-show meet-and-greets. Haley's appearance on tour was generating buzz, and we wanted to film another video featuring her as a special bonus surprise for the fans. We had a day off coming up in Switzerland, and we decided to film it then.

On March 15, 2015, we visited 571 Recording Studio in Zurich, Switzerland, to record three videos, one of which was "Creep." Like a comet, that video took off in a way that none of ours had done before. It didn't receive hundreds of thousands of views right off the bat, as we'd seen happen with "Thrift Shop" and "Royals"; instead, its momentum built slowly, as people around the world shared it with their friends. The view count increased day after day, and our version of "Creep" eventually soared right into the hearts of several major news outlets, including the *Los Angeles Times*, which hailed it "Cover of the Year." Haley had people all over the world talking: Fans who remembered her from her *American Idol* years loved seeing mainstream media taking notice of her stunning voice, and others who were hearing that voice for the first time became instant fans. My popularity rose, too—further confirmation of how beneficial the collaborative process and giving each other the space to grow and glow can be—and record labels, TV producers, and great singers the world over were reaching out. I was no longer just the outsider or the weirdo I had always felt myself to be. And yet, in a way, I still was and would always be; that Haley and I had the courage to embrace our inner outcasts played, I believe, no small part in the success we achieved.

SUCCESS (AND ITS DISCONTENTS)

was at South Beverly Grill, sitting through yet another lunch meeting with yet another group of major record label executives. They were wearing crisp, bespoke suits and expensive watches; I was wearing a nice watch myself, just to let them know I meant business, and I made sure to flash it in such a way that it caught the light. To my left was Jaron, who did most of the talking. To my right was Rook, who was working as my assistant. He was taking notes on a legal pad but also drawing funny pictures. All three of us had just ordered more sushi because we knew the label execs would be picking up the tab. Some things never change.

After years of breaking down doors to try to get people to listen to me, it's nice to be on the other side, I thought to myself.

Successful is a relative term. You can be considered successful by your peers and not feel accomplished at all if you're constantly comparing yourself to the world's most influential people. If you've ever thought that your happiness levels would radically change with success, I can assure you with complete certainty that you're wrong. Sure, you may experience some temporary spikes in happiness, but after a while, it will return back to its baseline level, just like always. Once upon a time, I found it baffling that people who seemingly had it all could ever be anything less than happy with their lives, but getting to the other side gave me a new perspective. If anything, more extreme highs make the lows that much harder to handle. And since past success doesn't guarantee future success, chances are high that there *will* be lows.

The road to success is often a desolate and lonely one. To truly dedicate yourself to a project requires that everything else in your life temporarily take a back seat. Personal relationships suffer. Leisure time is forfeited. Even sleep becomes an inconvenience.

Initially, my experiences with success were nothing but positive. At events and shows, everyone went out of their way to accommodate me and make sure I was enjoying myself. Companies sent me free products in the hopes that I would plug them online. My reality seemed to have a filter on it that removed all negative interactions with people. And while I wasn't *famous* famous, I would occasionally get recognized by total strangers, which was usually pretty flattering and thrilling...save for slightly disappointing exchanges like this one:

PERSON ON THE STREET: Hey! I know you!
ME: Oh? Are you a fan of Post—
PERSON: YOU PLAY PIANO FOR THE CLOWN!
ME: Yep, that's me.

Back at my table at South Beverly Grill, however, everyone was well acquainted with my work and knew who I was. They showered me with compliments, gushing over how I was shepherding in a new era of classic entertainment and building a cutting-edge platform for discovering and breaking new artists. Jaron nodded in agreement, then told them they didn't know the half of what we had planned for the future. Rook was still taking notes but also hitting the sake pretty hard. I liked having these two at meetings with me; they felt like family.

My actual family was very proud of me, but they were naturally a bit worried about how big this project was becoming. My life, lately, had been anything but simple, and to my parents—two people who had always embraced a life of simplicity—this was cause for concern. A barrage of contracts hit my inbox daily as new shows were added to our schedule. Large sums of money flowed in and out of my company account as checks came in from shows, music sales, and the occasional song placement. On a holiday visit back East in late 2015, my parents noted that I seemed distracted, as though I wasn't really fully present. Defensively, I wanted to show them that they just didn't understand the magnitude of the project I was dealing with, so I sat them down, and we did the math: I was on track to earn more in a year than my parents had in their lifetimes.

"Our son is rich," my mom uttered aloud, though in more of a concerned than exuberant manner. The stakes for this project had gone way up, and what had started off as a fun hobby was now a high-risk business with dozens of employees, whose very livelihoods depended on the project's continued success. My parents knew that with that development came even greater pressure to succeed. It was a far cry from the simple life we'd enjoyed when I was growing up.

I grew used to being congratulated on my success by friends and family, but any time I felt like I had finally, just maybe, "arrived," the goalposts would move, and a shinier milestone would appear for me to set my sights on. I was eager to see what the future held, and so for the time being, at least, I was generally able to keep this pressure in check. There was a part of me, though, that recognized this wasn't going to be a sustainable way of life for very long.

MAKING IT WITHOUT
A RECORD DEAL

When I was in my twenties, all I wanted was a record deal. Being "signed" sounded so impressive. I fantasized about going back to New Jersey and being able to tell people around town with a cool nonchalance that I was a major label recording artist. Having a label spend a whole bunch of money to help me make art and then spend even *more* money to get that art in front of people sounded like a dream situation.

I know I'm not alone in having thought this way. Lots of artists wonder how to get a record deal, as though everything is easy street after that one hurdle is cleared. The fact of the matter is that if you *need* a record deal, you won't get one—at least not anymore. Today, being a talented singer, a great songwriter, or an innovative composer just isn't enough to land a major label deal. Today's labels are looking for safe bets with proven track records of ticket sales. In fact, most of the great artists from the past that we love probably would not have gotten record deals in today's market. It's important to understand this because many assume that record deals are just awarded to the most talented individuals. The modern-day record industry excels at expanding upon existing commercial success, but it's no longer interested in nor deft at scooping up raw, unknown talent and sculpting superstars.

Now, this may be the new reality, but how you choose to act in light of it is squarely on you. You can lament what's lost and rue the artless machine that has supplanted a once innovative recording industry, which is a line of thinking I've fallen victim to, but it never leads anywhere useful. Or, you can forge a way forward, using today's technology to empower yourself and build a career that isn't dependent on a big record label.

Nearly all the tools that once gave record labels huge advantages over unsigned, independent musicians are now available to everyone the world over. Albums and singles can be recorded on a personal laptop and distributed on iTunes, Spotify, and other platforms with just a few clicks. Projects can bypass investors and a record label's recoupable advances against royalties with crowdfunding on sites like Kickstarter and Patreon, and fan bases can be established and marketed to for very little money on social media. The great paradox of the age we live in, then, is that it's one in which it's exceedingly difficult to secure a record deal, and yet pursuing the path of an independent musician has never carried with it more potential upside. Another way to look at it: For the first time in the history of recorded music, you now have the astounding ability to become your *own* record label.

Sometime after moving to Los Angeles, I found myself in the enviable position of being courted by multiple record labels. The part of me that could still viscerally recall the struggle of being a young musician was ecstatic, and the prospect of finally having my talent validated by the industry inflated me with hope. But the more I learned about the financials of the record deals on offer, the more it dawned on me that they might not be necessary for Postmodern Jukebox. You see, I'd singlehandedly invested and risked the money and sweat that an old-school label would have once provided to get PMJ to the level where we had millions of fans, and now I was making good money on digital sales *without* a label. Meanwhile, thanks to the complexities of what is actually referred to as "record label accounting," many of my friends with traditional deals had yet to see even a penny in royalties.

Jaron agreed that a traditional record deal just didn't make sense for me anymore. He even said as much during some of the label meetings we took, in part in order to prove this truth to me:

JARON: So, to cut right to it, a traditional label deal just doesn't make any sense for us.

RECORD LABEL EXECUTIVE: (confused) So...what are we having this meeting for?

JARON: I just want you guys to *know* that we don't need you. My client has built a massive platform, and we're just skimming the surface of what's possible. This thing is going to be fucking *huge.*

RECORD LABEL EXECUTIVE: Well, it was nice hearing about what you're doing.

JARON: Sure thing—thanks for dinner.

Of course, if you're comfortable giving up some creative control in exchange for a better chance at big-time fame, then signing a record deal might not be the worst move for you. Certainly, if you're looking to be a Top 40 artist, your best bet is to sign with a major label and work with the writers and producers the label recommends. Terrestrial radio is still king in the Top 40 world, and the major labels have virtually a monopoly on radio. Modern record labels are built around the goal of producing hit singles for artists, which in turn drive ticket sales and lead to sponsorships, TV and film appearances, and other moneymaking content.

If you do choose to go it alone or team with an independent

label, you can still make albums, tour, land sponsorships, and strike licensing deals. If you enjoy having an active role in business dealings, you might prefer to act as your own label and hire people to perform the various duties that labels provide their artists. When you're your own record label, you can do things the way you want, whenever you want.

My advice to artists is not necessarily to avoid record deals but to instead imagine that you may never get the opportunity to sign one. How would you release your music? How would you build a following? How would you make money? These are not rhetorical questions. Rather, they're questions whose answers will guide your creative efforts—and eventually your future.

ENGAGE, CROWDFUND, RELEASE, MONETIZE

If you're starting from scratch, there's a very basic cycle to follow that I still use to this day: Engage, crowdfund, release, monetize, repeat. Each time you go through this cycle, you have the opportunity to make new fans, make more money, and further develop your career as an artist. You also get a chance to find out firsthand what works and what doesn't, which in turn allows you to optimize the cycle for better results.

Engagement refers to all the different ways you draw in your existing fans, which also includes friends and family. (In fact, when I was just starting out, they were the only fans I had!) To engage your fans, start by showing them something that might be of interest to them. Examples include sharing a video of you playing a snippet of a song on social media, or posting a poll and leaving it up to your followers to decide what kind of video you will make, or starting a discussion about something that is important to you and possibly to them, too. Engaging your fan base means building a connection, so that they feel invited to go on a journey with you. This more than any other step is the key to launching any successful project because no success can happen without fans first being engaged. Some people—perhaps especially those of us who are private—might feel more resistance to this than others, but you don't need to completely unload your personal life on display for public consumption. You just need to show people that you're a unique talent with unique and interesting preoccupations. Over the years, my own efforts to engage fans have taken the form of everything from asking fans to Photoshop funny pictures of me to curating a series of reviews of (inevitably disappointing) airport lounges.

Crowdfunding is very simply the way of the future for financing creative projects. For artists who are uncomfortable asking their fans for things, this doesn't necessarily have to translate into "give me money so I can make stuff." Crowdfunding can also be done in the form of more traditional sales items, like an album preorder or a special deluxe package. In fact, the only difference between crowdfunding an album and selling it through a traditional channel is that with crowdfunding, the selling takes place upfront. Because of that—and because people are more tentative about spending money on a product they can't yet see or sample—I always seek to be as specific as possible when announcing a crowdfunding project. Share your inspiration for the project, your vision, and a rough timeline. The more that people can get a clear picture of what you're trying to achieve, the more likely they are to pledge their support.

Of all the steps in the cycle, *release* is the one that takes the most effort. That's because it involves putting together the project you've spent weeks just talking about doing. If you're a perfectionist like I used to be, you already know how I feel about that: Keep those tendencies in check! If you have trouble seeing projects through, it may help to use some of the crowdfunding money to hire a producer who can keep you on track. A project that is fifty, seventy-five, or even ninety-five percent done doesn't count as a release. To complete this step, you must find a way to follow through.

Monetizing can be as basic or complex as you allow it to be. An upside of crowdfunding is that you will (hopefully) already be out of the red by the project's completion; if that's the case, any extra sales you make will just be icing on the cake. Use the surplus to help fund the next project, or to buy falafel sandwiches, or whatever. If your project is a song or an album, you can monetize it by listing it on iTunes, Amazon, Bandcamp, etc. If it's a video, you can monetize it by running ads with it on a site like YouTube or by selling—via the many online outlets that let you upload your design and/or logo to a variety of templates and unbranded items—merch that ties in to your project's release. Think everything from t-shirts, hats, beer coozies, and bottle openers to temporary tattoos, pins, phone cases, underwear—whatever. If your creation takes the form of text, sell it online worldwide as an e-book. In today's on-demand marketplace, the goods being sold are only produced when a customer places an order for them. The site takes a cut of your sales, but in return it handles all the logistics, production, and shipping of the merch. What's especially great is that, because you're not stocking any inventory, you don't run the risk of overestimating consumer interest and winding up with negative earnings and boxes upon boxes of unsold boxer shorts in your living room.

If you think your project has the potential to take off in a big way, you can support it with an outside marketing and publicity firm to expand its reach, though that's not always necessary. If you're just starting out, I suggest setting a successful completion of the cycle for the first time as your goal.

Once you've successfully engaged your fan base, crowdfunded an idea, and released and monetized a project, it's nice to take a second to congratulate yourself...before getting right back to work. The system can help you build a foundation for a career, but if you stop for too long and lose momentum, it will be harder to get the engagement level back up again. If I learned one thing from our initial money-losing and break-even tours, it's that worrying too much about sales figures or end results can lead you to make suboptimal short-term decisions. Just celebrate the fact that by moving through the cycle and doing what you love, you're officially an *artist*.

When artists who are brilliantly talented but clueless about how to find and reach their audience without a record deal come to me for advice, I frequently tell them Morgan James' story. Through dedication, intelligence, and a willingness to engage with her fans, she used the Postmodern Jukebox platform as a jumping-off point to build a platform of her own, one that could take her as far as she wants to go. Whereas many artists are passively reactive, waiting for other people to discover *them* and build a following *for* them, Morgan was decidedly proactive in making things happen for herself. She understood that, at the end of the day, she was the only person responsible for her career.

When her Postmodern Jukebox videos and tour appearances began to put her in front of millions of people, Morgan looked for ways to turn Postmodern Jukebox fans into fans of Morgan James as well. Her YouTube channel had a small but dedicated following, which she grew by regularly posting covers, acoustic performances, and behind-the-scenes footage. On Facebook and Instagram, she uploaded engaging photos from her travels and interacted with her fans. When PMJ was touring, she was often the cast member to linger the longest in the lobby after a show, signing autographs and giving out cards with her upcoming dates so that fans could keep in touch with her. She knew the importance of maintaining a personal connection with a fan base, and she also knew how to allow fans to help her achieve her dreams.

Morgan came back from our Europe tour with a fivefold increase to her Facebook fan following, and her appearances on our North American tour generated even more buzz. Night after night, as she sang "Take Me to Church," she had the crowds holding their breath, mesmerized. By the summer of 2015, she had amassed a following of more than a hundred thousand people and was headlining shows of her own across the country.

If being consistently involved with your fans over a long period of time is one way to build a following, then strategic impatience is another. The performers who successfully make the jump from Postmodern Jukebox to their own solo careers—and there have now been quite a few of them—all have that quality of restlessness about them. What we're told as children about the value of "waiting our turn" doesn't necessarily hold true when you get off the playground and into the world of adults. Waiting around in the hopes of being discovered as an artist has never been a good strategy. Go ahead and *be impatient*. We only have thirty thousand days on this planet, give or take, and the typical life span of a career in music is a small fraction of that. You don't need to do the math to get the message: There's not enough time to be wasting it waiting for someone else to decide when you're up for your time in the spotlight.

Whenever you hear "it'll never work," in response to an idea you might have, take it for what it is: a challenge. Standing out from the crowd requires real mental toughness, and if you can't stand up for yourself when people try to shame you into abandoning your dreams, you'll never be prepared to face the obstacles that come your way when you finally do start to experience success. When someone challenges your vision in a way that doesn't sit right with you, don't waste your time arguing with them or trying to change their mind. Instead, thank them for their concern and just continue on your journey.

SETTING UP SHOP

Although PMJ's touring operation wasn't yet profitable, the recording side of things certainly was. Helped by the viral success of "Creep," I was getting large checks from digital sales and streams each month in 2015. It had become increasingly clear to me that Postmodern Jukebox was the only record label I needed. My team—which had grown to include a social media department and a marketing expert—and I wound up handling pretty much all the functions of a larger, formal record label anyway. Like the A&R divisions of the past, we identified singers, dancers, and musicians with talent and developed them into artists with followings—artists who could then go on to release albums and mount tours of their own. Whereas the major labels would only take existing success and magnify it, PMJ was building artists from scratch and helping them find the success they deserved. My job as a producer was to identify the qualities of a particular performer that made the person unlike any other performer on the planet and then conceive of a unique and attention-grabbing way to showcase them.

I'll be the first to admit that Postmodern Jukebox Productions wasn't the most creative name I could have given the label, but I'll also be the first to defend that what we were doing was anything but traditional. We had only one act—Postmodern Jukebox—fronted by an array of vocalists. We weren't interested in chart position or trying to capture the youth market; indeed, a large percentage of our fans were over age forty, and we were just fine with that. We didn't even have a mailing address because at this point in my life, I was technically without a home...*again*.

After returning from our second European tour, I figured I'd just stay in a hotel for a week, while I looked for a new place to rent. Before I knew it, that week had turned into a very expensive month. The problem was, most of the places that fit my unusual living specifications—no neighbors and a room big enough to host an entire band and sound and lighting equipment—were either cost-prohibitive or extremely far from civilization. Fortunately, just when I had memorized the entire Courtyard Marriott menu, I received a tip about a four-bedroom house in Tarzana, California, conveniently located at the top of a hill. Despite some weird architectural choices, such as a hot tub situated smack in the middle of the master bedroom, it was perfect. A couple days later, I signed the lease and made it official: PMJ had itself some fancy new digs.

Bro Mountain—as it was dubbed by Mykal during the filming of one of his videos there—lived up to its testosterone-drenched moniker. My longtime friends Rook, Adam, and Chip moved into the spare rooms, and the property soon became part music studio, part college dorm (even though we were all in our thirties). We bought an old Nintendo console and spent too much time trying to beat the game *Jackal* (while learning its theme music in the process, of course—music nerd habits die hard). We projected movies onto the side of the house in a recurring series we referred to as "Hot Tub Theatre." Adam even decorated his room with the same posters he'd had on the wall of his bedroom during high school. I joked that we were living like the

TV show *Entourage*, except on a much tighter budget. Between Rook's crazy schemes, Adam's quick-witted snark, and Chip's goes-down-easy charisma, we regularly got ourselves way too deep into situations we never should have been in in the first place, but boy was it fun.

As it usually goes when the rent isn't cheap, however, there came a point when the fun didn't need to stop, exactly, but it did need to subside just enough that it wasn't all we were doing. I had found a creative home base for our operation; now it was time to get to work making arrangements for our next tour, which would take us on a more extensive journey through North America—our first truly major U.S. tour. Always at the ready with a pun, Rook named this one the "Great Impression Tour," since it would be our chance to do what we had done already in Europe: establish ourselves as an important touring act. I added a publicist to the team to help us get press coverage at the shows, and I began rewriting the show based on what I had learned from working with the cast in Europe. In touring—as in all other aspects of life—first impressions are extremely important.

Casting this tour was much easier than the previous one had been. In her time away from the group, Robyn had made great strides to establish herself as a solo artist and launch a vintage YouTube channel of her own, using the same concept that I had employed. To the delight of her fans, she was now back touring with us, with a newfound confidence. We also had two new, noteworthy additions to the PMJ family: tap dance sensation Sarah Reich and powerhouse vocalist Maiya Sykes.

As I had many other PMJ stars, I met Sarah through Shoshana Bean, the Broadway legend who had become something of an older sister to PMJ. I was looking for a tap dancer to perform at our Hyde residency, and Shoshana had practically screamed Sarah's name, so I figured she was a safe bet. Sarah arrived at rehearsal the day of the show and very calmly proceeded to demonstrate the most impressive tap dancing I had ever seen in my life. Her rhythm was impeccable, effortless, and swung hard.

Sarah was barely in her mid-twenties but was already an extremely accomplished performer—not to mention that she'd also, by this point in time, built a worldwide community of talented up-and-coming tap dancers through her own group, the Tap Music Project. When she joined us at our Hyde residency, she effortlessly stole the show.

Our 1920s-style remake of "Bad Romance" was the first PMJ video to feature Sarah's amazing talent, in this case set alongside Ariana Savalas' lead vocal. To really make a spectacle of her PMJ debut, we released the video on the same day as her first tour appearance with us. Both our online and in-person audiences were smitten, instantly won over by Sarah as she pulled off one seemingly impossible tap step after another, grinning mischievously all the while. She was PMJ's very own tap-dancing Tinkerbell.

Maiya came to us at Shoshana's recommendation, too, during our Hyde residency. Her own performance of "Creep"—powerful, plaintive, and proud—had blown the roof off Hyde just before we left for Europe, and the upcoming U.S. tour felt like the perfect place to debut her. The daughter of two musicians, she started performing young, touring for years with big names like Neil Diamond and Macy Gray before making a much-lauded appearance on *The Voice*.

And her voice was just one part of her multifaceted talent. Maiya was also a skilled writer, vocal arranger, and music educator who had triple-majored at Yale and later completed graduate studies at Oxford. When anything went wrong onstage, her quick thinking enabled her to steer the band in a new direction, skillfully and gracefully.

Just as had been the case with the European tour, the cast for the upcoming Great Impression Tour was a diverse mix of old friends and new talents. After a few days of rehearsing in Brooklyn, we climbed aboard the big blue tour bus—our home base on wheels for the next couple months. We spent that first night sitting up late, swapping stories and project ideas. It reminded me of the first day of school; even for this former angsty teen, there had always been a certain optimism in the air at the start of a new year, in a new grade, with all its implied promise of adventures to be had and friendships to be fostered. As the bus rolled on through the night on its way to Boston, one by one we retired to the womb-like bunks and slept, dreaming of the possibilities that awaited us.

MAKING A GREAT
IMPRESSION

The loose, largely improvised feel of the Postmodern Jukebox stage show served us well on our first several tours. During that time, we experimented with new material, set lists, and even show formats, all the while using our audiences' reactions and feedback to gauge how we were doing. As we embarked on our most ambitious tour yet—a trip through the mainland United States at the largest venues we'd ever played—that loose approach wasn't going to cut it. The promoters were taking a risk by putting us in spacious performing arts centers instead of small clubs, and we had to prove—through consistent and reliable delivery of smooth, professionally executed performances— that we belonged alongside the successful touring acts that came through such venues. I was confident, however, that the high level of musicianship and creativity we presented onstage would more than compensate for a lack of experience. After all, we were here to shake the music industry up—not adhere to its rigid standards.

Our first stop was Boston, where we'd be playing at the Wilbur Theatre. Unlike most of our other venues, the Wilbur was larger and seated, and tickets were accordingly pricier. The audience wasn't just coming to see some of their favorites from YouTube;

they were here to experience a *show*. Backstage, I gave my best motivational speech to the cast; we had lots of talented people on tour, and I was determined to show the crowd what we could do.

Now, in a smaller, standing-room venue, the mere act of being onstage can generate the kind of frenetic energy that carries a show all the way through to the end. In a seated performing arts center, the energy from the crowd doesn't reach the stage, which leaves the performers feeling much more exposed. Any slight mistake or late entrance seems magnified in this setting. Despite all the great performers, the evening had its share of rough moments and pacing hiccups; I hadn't quite figured out yet how to properly tailor our performances for a seated and more mature crowd, and it showed.

There were other logistical challenges, too. We had set up a pre-show meet-and-greet for VIP ticket holders, which enabled them to come watch the sound check and meet the cast. What hadn't been factored in was that this was scheduled for 5 p.m., and the performers typically didn't get into hair and makeup until after dinner. In fact, many of them used the afternoon to exercise and then would arrive to sound check in their gym clothes. As a result, the VIPs who had been so excited to meet us that night at the Wilbur were treated to some very interesting photos, in which they were invariably dressed far better than the performers. It was a bit awkward for all parties involved, and conditions didn't improve much when Rook began filling the time our VIP guests spent waiting for the cast to arrive by telling "jokes" like this one:

ROOK: Why do interior designers hate flying?
VIP GUESTS: (silence)
ROOK: Because it's so *plane*.
VIP GUESTS: (more silence)

It was definitely a realistic peek behind the curtain, but our held-together-with-duct-tape aesthetic wasn't always appreciated.

One major factor that contributed to these planning slip-ups was that I wasn't used to running a tight ship. As a jazz musician, I was accustomed to just winging it and frequently suggested that others do the same. This had served me well in the past, but it was looking like it was time to reassess my approach and grab the reins a little tighter. People who pay good money for ticketed seats expect polish and a sense of security, not production values that, as one displeased older audience member put it, "resembled a high school musical."

After initially viewing the complaints with defensiveness, I began to see that many of them had merit. Our fans were incredibly excited about this new type of entertainment, and it was frustrating to them when the entire experience didn't reach its obvious potential. As the tour continued, I wisely sought more help with organization and overall logistics, and Jaron and his associate Jordan flew out to several shows to watch from the audience's perspective and give critical feedback.

I was obviously a bit sad to scrap Talent Corner from our soundchecks, but the extra fifteen minutes we saved allowed us to spend more time troubleshooting certain elements of the show. One obvious problem that Jaron and Jordan identified was that our technical specifications called for a fixed spotlight, and on each show—without fail—one of our singers would somehow end up a couple of feet off the mark, effectively delivering their song in darkness. We simply had the singers practice "finding their light" in soundcheck, and before long, they were hitting the marks consistently.

To address the flaws in the meet & greet comedy-hour, we decided to move the entire experience post-show. Now VIP fans got the chance to meet and congratulate the performers in full wardrobe, which killed the previous awkwardness and made the pictures come out that much better. Little by little, the complaints dwindled and the overall show feedback quickly went from good to great. Our tour had found its rhythm.

We sold out big shows at Nashville's Cannery Ballroom, the Vic in Chicago, and Crystal Ballroom in Portland. Fans were recognizing us on the street and stopping us for photographs. The cast was enjoying the creature comforts that came with a higher-profile tour, too. The cramped and dirty dressing rooms of tours past had been replaced by more lavish accommodations. Even our bus had been upgraded significantly, with mood lighting and a slide that expanded the square footage when parked.

At last, we seemed to be making a great impression on our U.S. audiences, and it felt fantastic. Positive reviews of the show circulated in influential industry magazines like *Pollstar*, and ICM was getting a slew of offers from new promoters excited to bring PMJ to their cities. The last stop on the tour, conveniently, was home: close to twenty-five hundred people attended our Los Angeles show at Club Nokia—our biggest crowd to date. It was overwhelming in the best way possible; we were mobbed by fans after the show, until venue security showed up to escort us from the building. Times like this never felt completely real to me, and perhaps they weren't.

The next morning, when I went for my usual run from my house down to The Coffee Bean to get breakfast, no one recognized me or seemed to care that I was there. It was jarring. I thought about the jazz musicians I idolized; to me, they were larger than life, almost inhuman. I wondered if this was their experience, too, with *making it*—equal parts life-changing and mundane.

THE ADVANTAGES
OF AN ENTOURAGE

cotty! Come out here real quick!"

I muted my phone for a second. "Can't right now, guys, I'm on the phone."

"It's really important. Just ten seconds."

"All right, all right, hang on." I sighed, then unmuted my phone. "Uh—hey, can I call you right back? By the way, this online store idea's great, can't wait to hear more."

I walked through the sliding glass door and into the hot Tarzana sun. Rook and Adam were at the edge of the pool in matching Speedos. The pool deck was littered with cans of Pabst Blue Ribbon.

"Me and Kubota came up with our own YouTube show—*MASTERS OF DIVE!!*"

With that, Rook jumped off the diving board and pantomimed a karate chop as Adam blasted Metallica's "Master of Puppets" from a small stereo. The water shook violently, forming a tidal wave that sprayed outside the pool, taking a few beer cans in its wake. Rook and Adam roared with laughter.

I shook my head and turned around to head back into the house. "Well done, guys."

Indeed, the people you surround yourself with will become the most important people in your life. If that thought doesn't scare you *too* much, you're probably doing it right. As I gained access to more exclusive parts of society, I realized that many of the people I was being put in touch with had self-serving motives for wanting to work with me. Your friends, if you pick wisely and are lucky enough, can be a buffer against these sorts of people. Your *entourage*—in addition to being useful in sniffing out the snaky characters—can also make life a hell of a lot more fun than going it alone. When I found myself at parties with celebrities and CEOs and the like, I usually wound up just hanging with my friends and making dumb jokes instead of networking. In part, this was because I still hadn't shaken the pinch-me feeling that I'd snuck into this exclusive world and would eventually be outed as an imposter. The other part is that it takes me a long time to trust people. So, instead of making new friends, I did the opposite: I brought all my old friends with me. Trusted old friends, I found, can also make for awesome collaborators.

A prime example of one such friend-turned-PMJ collaborator is the extraordinary singer/songwriter and indie darling Nicole Atkins. We first met back at *Sleep No More*, when she was singing with the house band and I was the show's music director. Even then, I recall being taken by not only her vocals but her awe-inspiring stage presence as well. She may have been singing jazz standards, but Nicole was a rock star. She worked the stage, throwing her entire body into the performance. Outside work, she was down-to-earth, friendly, and candid about her weaknesses, in particular her struggle with alcoholism. The day after performing with me at one particularly boozy, slightly off-the-rails late-night set at the Manderley Bar, she called me to apologize and own the fact that she needed to get some help. The apology was wholly unnecessary, but I was concerned for her, and I hoped that she would follow through on getting help—for her own sake. She had such a good heart, and her boundless talent was deserving of far wider recognition; it would be a shame to see her addiction hinder her.

It wasn't until several years later, shortly after I'd moved to Tarzana, that Nicole let me know that she was coming to town, newly sober and ready to channel all of her energy into performing. This was music to my ears.

When Nicole arrived, it was clear she was in a much better place. We discussed how life was too short not to cherish it completely and then began talking about David Bowie's recent death and how we both had watched people dear to us face cancer. We hit upon the idea of covering Bowie's "Heroes" and donating the first week's sales to the Cancer Research Institute. I hastily scribbled out a chord chart, and with the help of Adam on bass and Chip on drums, composed an arrangement on the spot. It was the least amount of time ever spent on a Postmodern Jukebox arrangement, but with Nicole at the mic, I was confident it would be great nonetheless.

It takes a singer of Nicole's caliber to really make you feel the lyrics of a song like "Heroes." Her performance started out restrained and almost whisper-like, but by the end she was picking the microphone stand off the ground to belt out "We can beat them forever and ever!" The recording went on to be prominently featured in an anti-drunk-driving campaign starring Formula One champion Jackie Stewart. Weaving in classic footage of Stewart through the years—and ending with an appearance by Stewart himself—the video was widely praised as a cinematic feat, and Nicole's heartfelt vocals made it all the more impressive. With so many things going right for us—our own freestanding space for recording (noise complaints no more); a growing network of very fine collaborators, old and new; better equipment than we'd ever been able to afford in the past; and the California sun melting away our stresses—we were perfectly positioned to produce some major hits. We continued to film all the new videos at the house, having modified the living room to include an Austrian drape backdrop, a checkerboard floor, and a new lighting rig. Being able to walk downstairs and step right onto the PMJ set made the environment feel much more relaxed. The drama of the previous year had largely dissipated, and for once, I was finding balance in my life. I also had another reason to be happy: I had begun dating a dancer named Natalie Rose White.

A Brit who grew up in Cornwall, Natalie was not only beautiful, she also had an upbeat manner and dry sense of *humour* that I found magnetic. Living in LA, it often felt like whenever I went out, no matter *where* I went, phony Hollywood types abounded. Natalie kept me grounded and reminded me of who I was and where I came from, just like my entourage of old friends did. She didn't care about fame or money or social media influence; she liked *me*, the person. It was refreshing and a great counterbalance to my workaholic tendencies. That she was an innovative and playful choreographer was the icing on the cake. Natalie helped enhance a few of our newest videos with her work, and her choreography helped inspire a new emphasis on visuals and *blocking*—the precise staging of performers throughout a show—in our touring productions.

This era of entourage advantages also helped produce two massive hits for PMJ. Haley Reinhart, who was by now a prime attraction on tour, recorded her first video at Bro Mountain: a bluesy, dirge-inspired remake of The White Stripes' "Seven Nation Army," featuring her cooing and growling alongside a plunger-muted New Orleans horn section. Mykal, our star emcee in Europe, paid us a visit stateside so we could record a couple new tunes, one of which went on to become a bona fide hit and tour standard: a '50s-style remake of "My Heart Will Go On," the love ballad from the movie *Titanic*, originally performed by Céline Dion.

Our take on "My Heart Will Go On"—influenced by the type of love songs that Jackie Wilson used to sing—caught fire online as soon as we released it. Kate Winslet, Ashton Kutcher, and even Céline Dion herself shared it on social media. It was vocally stunning, creative, and extremely danceable—in essence, Postmodern Jukebox at its best. A few months later, the video helped Mykal land a role on NBC's musical television special *The Wiz Live!* alongside big names like Queen Latifah, Mary J. Blige, and David Alan Grier.

Mykal wasn't the only PMJ artist to experience wider recognition. One day, Jaron emailed me to tell me that folks at Extra gum—after watching "Creep"—were interested in having us record a popular Elvis standard with Haley for one of their ad campaigns. Since doing covers of older material wasn't exactly what Postmodern Jukebox was known for, we agreed to put Extra in touch with Haley directly so that she could take charge of the project herself. The resulting recording—a stripped-down version of the Elvis classic "Can't Help Falling in Love," with Casey on piano—went on to feature prominently as the soundtrack of an award-winning sentimental campaign titled "The Story of Sarah & Juan." The single caught on, massively, and as of this writing, it's sold over a hundred thousand units—certified gold.

Of course, nobody could stop talking about the beautiful voice that infused the track with so much emotion: *Was it the singer who sang "Creep" with PMJ?* Haley had become a superstar, and little by little, my Postmodern Jukebox entourage was evolving into a robust, full-fledged community of prolific talent.

No matter how high the success stories stacked up, we were careful to never let them turn us pretentious or self-serious. We knew that the anything-goes vibe at the heart of PMJ was our special sauce; no way were we going to let it subside. Between recording madcap videos at home and playing shows to thousands of people, we still managed to find the time to get ourselves into a multitude of absurd situations. Rook got kicked out of a karaoke bar after being deemed too drunk to finish his modified, much more risqué version of the Baha Men classic "Who Let the Dogs Out?" Adam, in honor of our first summer pool party, bought us all matching Speedos, which obviously we gamely wore (much to Natalie's embarrassment). Indeed, if I had any pretentious leanings or ambitions, my entourage helped dispatch them swiftly.

In an effort to preserve all the friend memories and PMJ milestones, around this time we established what has since become our fabled "tour museum" in Bro Mountain's second floor common area—an absurdist collection of unusual artifacts from PMJ tour history, largely curated by Adam. Perhaps someday we'll open the collection to the general public and look on as our fans cycle through confusion and possibly disappointment in the face of so many seemingly random objects—think a "Merch Madness" poster featuring a Photoshop of Rook jumping out of a barrel or a disturbing X-ray of Casey's tooth after he went to the dentist for the first time in years—that really only have significance insofar as they remind *us* of our favorite inside jokes.

Life was great. I was surrounded by people who made me happy, and I was doing what I loved. I had achieved what felt like just the right level of fame—enough that I got to relish the occasional rock star moment but not so much that I risked becoming big-headed and losing sight of my sincere artistic values and reasons for creating. I felt like I could do this forever.

THE SEARCH
FOR FREEDOM

By the end of 2015, I was in an unprecedented position an as artist: I had complete control and ownership over every aspect of my art—every recording, every video, every show. Each day, I got to wake up and spend my time exactly as I decided: planning new videos, coming up with fresh bits for the show, and brainstorming songs for our singers that we hadn't covered already. I didn't have a boss breathing down my neck or rigid hours to conform to; I was blessed to not be dealing with any personal crises, and I was completely financially independent. The struggles in life that most people my age were dealing with—job security, debt, family issues—no longer applied to me.

On the surface, this no doubt looked a lot like freedom.

In reality, though, I *did* report in to a boss, one whose standards weren't always so easy to meet. That boss was none other than my own expectations for myself and the life-defining project that Postmodern Jukebox had become. And let me tell you, this boss was *relentless*.

The perfectionist monster that prevented me from reaching my potential earlier in life had returned, albeit this time convincingly disguised as something that—at first glance—looked a whole lot like healthy ambition. After all, I was on a roll. My YouTube subscriber count had surpassed the one million mark. PMJ was easily topping the iTunes jazz charts with each new album released. I was profiled in crème de la crème publications, including *Forbes, AdWeek,* and *Billboard.* On *The Voice,* Christina Aguilera pointed to our version of "Creep" as inspiration for a contestant, and other celebrities were declaring their love for PMJ. I played a Justin Bieber song with Broadway and television star Kristin Chenoweth on my Instagram.

As the act's fame grew, we found ourselves booking bigger and better venues, and in turn we rose to the occasion, pouring all our energy into making our shows increasingly elaborate and engaging. In London, we played two nights at the beautiful (and appropriately named) Roundhouse. In Los Angeles, we played the Microsoft Theatre, home to the *MTV Video Music Awards* and Kanye West's infamous announcement that he would run for president in 2020. I parodied this event onstage by announcing my own presidential bid, which went over well with the crowd; the mic drop I followed it up with, not so much . . . at least by the venue staff, who just stood shaking their heads in frustration. With the exception of Microsoft Theatre's sound techs that night, my talent—and the talent I'd passionately brought together under the umbrella of PMJ and encouraged and also benefited from— was being validated left and right, and it felt *good.*

But beneath the surface, the pressure was getting to me. Gone were the days of simply overseeing a YouTube channel. I now had a touring company, my own record label, and an online merch store, all with employees who directly reported to me. It had been a good ten years since I'd begun bringing others onto my team, and yet still, maddeningly, I couldn't grasp how to properly delegate tasks. When our social media managers posted to

Facebook, I would often go in and edit what they'd posted to better fit our brand aesthetic. When our promoters requested a promo video to help market our tour, I hired a company to create one and—unhappy with their results—just did it myself. I was clocking close to eighty hours per week on work, often waking up in the middle of the night to send emails and rewrite publicity materials—and that's when I *wasn't* on tour. My need for control had spiraled *out* of control.

On tour, the burden of my self-assigned, crazy-making work-load was even greater, as my need to micromanage every aspect of the project prevented me from ever relaxing. Although I still incorporated cast members' ideas into the show, I'd become quicker to shoot down ideas that didn't grab me immediately. I believed that I had earned the right to not have my judgment be questioned. I wasn't leading; I was dictator-ing.

The truth, I realized later, was that I was nowhere near as free as I believed myself to be. Freedom doesn't necessarily come from working for yourself, or from setting your own hours, or even from never having to worry about money. Freedom is a state of mind. It's the recognition that pursuing what modern celebrity culture has a way of telling us we *should* want in life—fame, fortune, accolades—will never lead to contentment. Freedom is about surrendering control and letting the chips fall where they may—and knowing that you'll be okay.

"Hey, Scotty, Jaron emailed me...the Aussie promoters changed the interviews, so as soon as you land, they're going bring you to the hotel so that you can do two hours of press."

I stopped packing and looked at Rook.

"Are you serious? It's a sixteen-hour flight, and I can never fall asleep on planes. I'll be exhausted. No way I'm doing that."

"Well, the promoters really need this to sell some more tick-ets. What should I tell them?"

"I don't know, tell them you'll impersonate me and do the interviews or something."

"Sounds good....I bet they'll be excited to hear Scott Bradlee's fancy new *Australian accent! G'DAY, SYDNEY!*" Rook said, delivering that last line in some bizarre hybrid of Cockney English and Cajun accents.

"Never mind...I'll do the damn interviews myself," I said wearily.

Suits? Check.

Phone charger? Check.

Laptop? Check.

Enough granola bars to keep me from racking up excessive hotel minibar charges? Check.

As I packed my suitcase for another month-long tour—this time of New Zealand, Australia, and Southeast Asia—I reflected on my early days of making YouTube videos in a small, dimly lit apartment in Astoria. I had nothing to lose back then, and it showed in the videos: They had a certain un-self-conscious spirit to them. I wasn't making things to please a mainstream audience; I was making them for myself. I was doing what I loved. Every time I set up the camera and hit the red Record button, I felt the exhilarating rush of discovery.

Things weren't quite the same now. The last few videos I made before leaving for the PMJ: Down Under tour were rushed and came across more as attempts to keep a deadline than as the products of profound, undeniable inspiration. Worse, fans were noticing, and they let me know as much in the comments.

"This channel just doesn't do it for me anymore" read one comment.

Then don't watch it, asshole, I thought of writing back, but thankfully stopped myself. Since when did YouTube comments get under my skin like this? What had happened to me?

As I rode to the airport, I couldn't help but wonder whether I had it all backward. Perhaps I'd had more freedom at the start of this journey, back when I was still playing restaurants, than I did now. Perhaps "freedom" was actually recording jazz covers of Nintendo theme songs with my friends, as Aunt Agatha served us five-gallon jugs of split pea soup and creditors left me voicemails that went unanswered.

The TSA agent examined my passport and smiled. "I follow you guys on YouTube," she said. "Congrats on all your success!"

THINKING OUTSIDE
THE JUKEBOX

You want to *WHAT?*"

I was on the phone with ICM, and they sounded incredulous, as if they were actually not sure whether or not I was joking.

As I said the words again, slower this time, I wasn't entirely sure either.

"I'm going to take myself off of the road."

Silence on the other end.

"So, Postmodern Jukebox is done with touring? After we've built a successful touring act? Is this what you *want?*"

"Postmodern Jukebox will still tour," I clarified. "*I* just won't be on the road. I'm the creative director. I need a schedule that allows me to be creative. Besides, this project is bigger than any one person. It's bigger than me."

Jaron, who was also on the phone, predictably and excitably broke the silence. For once, I was relieved.

"We're going to build something that no one has ever built before. FUCKING. NO. ONE. This isn't a band. This is a chance to build a *global move—*"

"Jaron," Scott Mantell interjected, "are you expecting me to go to our promoters and sell them on the idea of a concert by Scott Bradlee's Postmodern Jukebox *without* Scott Bradlee?"

"That's precisely what I'm expecting you to do."

"You're crazy. You took an act from YouTube and turned them into a band that grosses millions, and now you want to just throw it all away. You know how rare success is in this business?"

It *was* crazy. I had taken creative risks my whole life, but this was the first time that something substantial hung in the balance: my entire career. I was by no means confident that my crazy plan would work, but something needed to give, and I was desperate. I knew that the only way for Postmodern Jukebox to reach its full potential—and the only way that I could have the energy to guide it there—would be if I stepped out of the spotlight and permitted it the space to grow into something exponentially bigger than me.

After the jet lag from our recent tour of Australia, New Zealand, and Southeast Asia subsided, it dawned on me: I didn't want to be a star. It had been a successful tour, but I closed it out feeling overextended, uncreative, and miserable. The sense of freedom that I'd naively believed I'd achieved just by having my name in lights was an illusion. Instead of free, I felt constantly confronted—by upset cast members who felt neglected; fans who didn't appreciate the videos I hurriedly put together between tours; press opportunities that demanded immediate attention; even belligerent hopefuls who would corner me after shows and sing at me in the hopes that I would cast them. I wanted to make everyone happy, but in trying to do so, I was stressing myself out and losing my temper at them instead.

I didn't want to be famous. I just wanted to have the space to be creative.

In the middle of one particularly rough week, feeling as though I'd reached my wit's end, I called Jaron. Sensing something was amiss, he just let me talk. As much as Jaron loved the sound of his own voice, he knew when to keep his mouth shut and listen.

"Remember how fun it was in the early days? When everything was new? When everything felt exciting? It's gone now. That feeling's gone. 'Make a video, go on tour, make a video, go on tour.' It's become *a job*. I feel so guilty for saying it, I really do, because I'm so grateful to have had this opportunity, but it does—it feels like a job."

I was expecting to be met by a pep talk filled with colorful language and questionable metaphors, like Jaron usually offered. But he seemed to be, shockingly, at a loss for words. I think he knew where I was coming from, having been a performing artist himself. It wasn't lost on me—or him—that he'd turned his back on performing right when he had a number one hit on country radio.

"Why don't you take a few days to think about it?" he countered, calmly. "And we'll go from there."

Worst pep talk ever, I thought and hung up, still frustrated.

Not five minutes went by before Jaron called back. "Why are we trying to force you into a box? You're not our accompanist, you're our fuckin' Walt Disney!"

Yep. The Jaron I knew and needed was definitely back.

"If the rules don't work for us, then we're gonna *break the rules*. What's been your goal with Postmodern Jukebox all along? What's the *big picture*?"

That was easy. "I want to spread it all over the world."

"Well, imagine if instead of taking ten years to do that, we could do it in five!"

I thought for a second.

"Wouldn't that require *more* shows?"

"YES!" he exclaimed. "But it doesn't matter, because we'll have *multiple casts on the road—all with different pianists and*

different bandleaders, executing your vision for the show. You could come to as many or as few shows as you wanted to. If you wanted to spend a month planning videos, you could do that. If you wanted to start a new project and needed six months off to do it, you could do that. Everything is built already. Now let's scale it and take it around the world."

It took a second to wrap my head around this. *Was this even possible?*

"So we'd put together multiple casts, rehearse them, and send them out. I wouldn't have to be on the road 24/7. And that way, we could get lots more of our performers out there, too."

"YES!" he screamed, accompanied by the sound of something shattering. "Fuck! I just knocked over my coffee."

Jaron had had an epiphany. He saw that I was holding myself back by attempting to do everything instead of just focusing on the things that only *I* could do. He'd also had a vision for how to grow Postmodern Jukebox so that it would reach more people around the world *and* expand its roster of performers. Best of all, PMJ would no longer run the risk of becoming an act with a short shelf life because we would constantly be bringing new and interesting talent to our fans. Suddenly, this was looking like something with the potential to last...*forever.*

The longer I thought about what Jaron was proposing, the more I realized that it wasn't just another way forward, it was the *only way* forward. The prospect of recapturing the creative freedom from those early days was incredibly enticing. No longer would I have to choose between writing arrangements and producing new remakes—the lifeblood of the project—and casting and touring. The two could happen in tandem. My main objective was ensuring that the show remained excellent, night after night, and that it retained the magic that's born from putting world-class performers together onstage.

The first step was to identify a great music director who understood the act. Todd Schroeder, who had done such an excellent job helping shoot our viral cover of "My Heart Will Go On," popped into my head right then. In addition to having a background similar to mine in ragtime and stride piano, Todd had been music director on shows for literally hundreds of Broadway and Hollywood stars—everyone from Tom Jones and Liza Minnelli to Jason Alexander and Josh Gad.

As we made the jump from small rock clubs to bigger theatres, Todd's background in Broadway proved to be a huge asset for us. Whereas concepts like blocking (telling performers where to move onstage, for visibility or dramatic effect) and lighting cues were foreign to me, they were both squarely in Todd's wheelhouse. He also knew how to build a set list into a dramatic presentation and maximize the impact of each song. Having proper song transitions creates contrast, the same way having proper lighting can highlight the features of a subject in a photograph. We began meeting regularly to pick apart the existing show's format to see what and where we could improve. One element that we both agreed should be increased was group numbers; despite having five superstar singers in any given show, only "Burn" and "All About That Bass" featured more than one vocalist. We also discussed giving members of the group more chances to interact with the audience; up to this point, most of the dialogue had been presented by the emcee, and the singers were paraded out silently (with the exception of Casey; we kind of let him do his thing, which at times involved him balancing a step ladder on his hand or wheeling himself around on a dolly, facedown, while introducing a song). We had a lot of vibrant characters on this tour, and we wanted the audience to feel like they knew each and every one of them personally by the show's end. Our goal was to build a show format that would best highlight the unique qualities of each cast member without elevating any one person over another.

The cast had recently seen some new additions, and we were eager to harness their various skills and strengths and fold them into the show. At the tender age of twenty-two but already with years of stage and TV experience, Sara Niemietz exhibited a rich, perfectly controlled alto beyond her years and masterful phrasing that recalled the jazz and soul hits of generations past. Aside from her obvious gifts, she also had the ability to light up a room with her positivity and enthusiasm—a tremendous asset when it comes to the often uncomfortable and physically draining experience of touring. It's hard to tell who loved Sara more—the audience or her fellow cast members.

Aubrey Logan was another newcomer recommended to me by Shoshana. "You *need* to work with her," she swore, by way of prefacing our introduction. And so Aubrey and I met up and did what seemed to be the natural thing to do: We recorded a jazz version of the *SpongeBob SquarePants* theme for my Instagram. She sang it the way Ella Fitzgerald would have sung it and capped it off with a trombone lick. I was reminded of something that day, which I'd learned back in my early days living in LA: Shoshana knows best.

I was impressed by Aubrey's talent from the get-go, but I discovered the true depths of that talent when we produced her debut video for PMJ: a quick jazz version of Taylor Swift's "Bad Blood." The original featured a couple rap verses by Kendrick Lamar, which I suggested we turn into some sort of bebop melody. Aubrey demoed the verses, transforming them into a rhythmically complex vocalese that could have come straight out of the horn of bebop legend Dizzy Gillespie. It was brilliant the way she used her voice as an instrument, effortlessly traversing its entire range. We expanded the arrangement and then brought in Adam on bass and Martin Diller on drums. It was a difficult arrangement, but the hardest part was coming up with a clever way to hand off to Aubrey a trombone to solo on after the bridge. In the end, we had Rook throw it to her—after checking to make sure it was fully insured. In the video, you can see that a brief flash of terror crossed Aubrey's face as the trombone hurtled toward her, but she quickly regained her composure in time to catch it and whip out a great solo.

When it came time for rehearsals, I gathered the cast—old and new—together and formally introduced them to Todd. Because of all the planned changes to the show format, I explained, rehearsals for the tour were going to be a lot more rigorous than they had been previously. Not everyone took to this development—particularly those who had been on the much looser, earlier tours and were accustomed to my (I like to think charmingly) disorganized management style.

TODD: So let's take a look at this script I wrote. The girls
 will read this line before "Burn—
THE CAST: We don't read lines in the shows, Todd.
TODD: Okay, well what *do* you do to fill the time while
 you're setting up for a song?
THE CAST: Scott told us to make stuff up on the spot and
 try not to be offensive.

If we were going to make this upgraded Postmodern Jukebox show work, we had to be willing to commit all the way—no half-assing, no cutting corners, no avoiding long-term change for the better just because it might be uncomfortable in the short term. Todd had his work cut out for him, but it would take much more than a little resistance from the cast to deter him. He was so in demand for a reason: He knew how to craft a show that held appeal for a wide variety of people, and he was patient. He was used to working with artists and knew that artists are often a bit possessive of their creations.

Even I was initially skeptical of his ideas, fearing that the show might veer a little too far to the "Broadway" end of things. But in the end, I came around to many of his suggestions, and Todd familiarized himself with my aesthetic preferences for PMJ. One of his ideas that I agreed to try was a duet to end the show: a mashup of "As Time Goes By" from *Casablanca* and the PMJ version of "Someday" by The Strokes. It would be a blend of old and new, a symbolic declaration, if you will, of the progressive future we had in store for Postmodern Jukebox. I was hesitant because we had traditionally ended the encore set with something upbeat and danceable—Mark Ronson's "Valerie" in the first tour and "Shake It Off" after that. But Todd's idea was to have the cast invite the audience to slow dance with one another and send them home with that special moment. The cast could even bring some audience members onstage to dance with them. It sounded a little schmaltzy to me, but I agreed to see if it took at our next show.

After finishing rehearsals in Brooklyn, we piled aboard the bus and set off for Baltimore for opening night at Meyerhoff Symphony Hall. Lots of the cast members were meeting for the first time, and we all stayed up late telling stories and generally getting to know one another. Something about the tour bus encourages deep conversations among relative strangers; it falls somewhere between a cocktail bar and a psychologist's couch, in terms of being this reliable—yet also magical—safe space, where airs are dropped, vulnerability is embraced, and everyone wears pajamas.

We arrived at the theatre—a major upgrade from even our last tour, with multiple dressing rooms and a rehearsal space with a piano—and went through our standard pre-show rituals: sound check, Talent Corner, dinner. When the show began, however, I didn't take my customary seat at the piano; I took a seat among the audience instead. It was going to be the first time I got to see a Postmodern Jukebox show from the audience's perspective, and I had butterflies in my stomach.

The show kicked off in blazing fashion, with a full cast performance of "Fancy" that concluded with a wicked tap solo by Sarah Reich and four-part cast harmonies. The crowd was rapt. Next, the show weaved through some of the fan favorites in the PMJ repertoire. I finally came onstage following "All About That Bass" and told a short version of the PMJ story before closing out with my usual crowdsourced piano mashup, an homage to my Robert Restaurant days. I'll admit, it was reassuring to receive the same exuberant applause as always, despite not being onstage the entire time. *I could get used to this,* I thought.

Watching the show from the audience was a surreal, almost out-of-body experience. Although I knew the arrangements inside and out, there was something magical about listening to the cast breathe new life into them night after night after night, from the audience's point of view. I imagine it's probably similar to what a screenwriter experiences when watching his or her script come to life as a movie: the feeling of managing to create a work that endures beyond oneself.

In those moments, I was watching as not just the show's creator but as a fan, too. I laughed when Casey went out into the audience to sing "Sweet Child o' Mine" to a darling elderly woman, and I held my breath during superstar emcee LaVance Colley's high notes in "Halo." Slowly, I felt my need to control every aspect of the show retreat, to be replaced by something far preferable: a peaceful sense of family. I wasn't alone in Postmodern Jukebox, and I didn't need to try to do everything single-handedly. I now had a family to build this universe with me.

At the start of the final encore, I took to the stage once more and played the intro of "As Time Goes By," while Cristina charmingly coaxed the audience to stand and encouraged them to dance with one another. Slowly but surely, everyone joined in—even our stage crew and the venue staff. It was a touching moment, and one that wound up feeling surprisingly sincere. We *were* all family. Backstage, we celebrated a great opening night with champagne.

While I was busy feeling like a proud parent, my own parents were bursting with pride over the new tour, which finally included a date near my hometown. They spent their first year in retirement watching every video, live stream, and bit of social media posted by every performer involved in the project. My mom in particular loved to research the performers and dig up interesting details about them—to her, it was reality TV *for real*.

It was with this loyal enthusiasm of my parents in mind that I planned an early morning tour bus stop at my parents' house, en route to our show in Bethlehem, Pennsylvania. The cast—which at this point included Casey, Haley, Sara, LaVance, and Todd—was tired from the previous night's show, but they managed to wake up in time to see the bus parked at the top of a driveway in rural Hunterdon County, New Jersey. Rook, naturally, had a video camera at the ready to capture my mom's reaction.

No sooner had the doors on the tour bus opened than we were greeted by the sight of my mom skipping up the driveway, like some five-year-old given rare permission to select a handful of sweets from a candy shop. She was excited to see me but maybe even more excited to see the performers she watched on her computer each day. She made little attempt to hide her excitement over meeting Casey, screaming upon recognizing him and hugging him.

"I LOVE YOU!!" my mom shrieked. She was the biggest fangirl.

"The love is mutual," Casey said.

After letting my mom make the rounds, we all trooped inside, where we spent the rest of the morning hanging out with my parents, having breakfast, and cracking up at all the awkward family photos of me from adolescence. Casey had fun perusing my parents' old record collection and gave our breakfast an impromptu '70s soundtrack.

After a truly chaotic year, this merging of my work family and my actual family was the bit of normalcy I was searching for. I didn't want to be famous; I wanted to hear my parents call me "Scotty," like they always had. I wanted to joke around with the cast and exchange childhood stories of rebellion. I wanted to create a place where we all belonged, where we could suspend time and the rush of the world outside, where we could be in awe of one another's talents and feel all those same feelings that I'd felt at thirteen, listening to a Louis Armstrong record that I'd recorded onto a cassette, off those same living room speakers we were now seated around.

For the first time in a long while, I felt strangely content.

THE SHOW MUST GO ON

Although I had successfully pulled myself out of the center of a creative crisis, my life was still far from stress free. Delegating so much responsibility to others meant that I wasn't always onsite when problems arose, and attempting to put out fires from afar, I found, was often even more nerve-wracking for me than being there in the thick of it. At the end of the day, my name was on the project, which ultimately made me responsible for whatever happened on the road—whether I was personally on that road too or not.

A particularly difficult set of problems arose during the three-day trip to Aspen, Colorado, that I made at the end of 2015. The most recent Postmodern Jukebox tour was slated to end there the next day, and I'd decided to take Natalie with me and arrive a day early, before the tour got there—a rare vacation. After all the challenges of the previous year, I was looking forward to taking a breather, for once, from being in constant work mode, and just enjoying some carefree winter fun.

The plane touched down and, like clockwork, I instantly turned on my phone to catch up on any emails I may have missed (old workaholic habits die hard—even on vacation). My phone buzzed with a veritable jackpot of notifications: four missed calls, three voicemails, and five text messages, mostly from Jaron. The most recent text of his just read "Call me ASAP." My stomach turned. *This can't be good.*

My gut instinct was correct. The touring cast had a show in Denver that night, but the bus was snowed in somewhere in Wyoming, with all outbound flights canceled. Oh yeah, and Joey Cook—the accordion-playing *American Idol* star who name-checked us on national television and had by now become a PMJ cast member—was in jail. It was a lot to process at the start of what was supposed to be a vacation.

The group was coming from a day in Rock Springs, Wyoming—a small town located just off I-80. The bus was scheduled to drive to Cheyenne, where I-80 met I-25, the interstate that led to Denver. But a sudden blizzard had forced closure of the highway, leaving nearby travelers stranded. Frustrating, but hardly surprising. This was, after all, the Great Northwest. When Will had explained the situation to me the day before, we'd agreed that our best bet was to ditch the tour bus and fly everyone into Denver early the next morning. It was a quick flight, and planes were still taking off, so the odds were in our favor.

And so while I was en route to Aspen, Will put the new plan into action. The cast and crew woke up extremely early, grabbed all their earthly possessions, and set out for the airport. The airport was small and empty except for a few other unlucky travelers. One by one, the sleepy tour party passed through security and congregated on the other side, antsy to board so that they could go back to sleep. It wasn't long before they noticed, however, that one of their peers hadn't made it through security: Joey.

It had been a rough tour for Joey. At twenty-two, Joey was our youngest cast member and by far the least experienced performer. She had gone straight from busking on the street to *American Idol* fame and had joined our group after recording some stellar videos with us at Bro Mountain. The breakneck pace of touring day after day was taxing on her vocal cords, and she fell ill within the first couple weeks.

Joey had a prescription for medical marijuana that was legal and recognized in her state, as well as in the flight's destination state of Colorado. However, marijuana, even for medicinal purposes, wasn't yet legal in Wyoming, and the small amount she had in her backpack was enough to get her in not-so-small trouble. She was summoned out of line at security, and like dark magic, a group of police with drug-sniffing dogs materialized. The color drained from her face when she realized what was happening. She was handcuffed and taken to jail, where she was told that the judge would be sentencing her the next day.

Meanwhile, everyone else (save for Will, who'd been called by Joey to come tend to the situation at the jail) had boarded the jet. They had been sitting there for nearly an hour, waiting for take-off, when an announcement came from the cockpit: The airplane was grounded indefinitely due to the weather and everyone would be deplaning. It was yet another item of bad news. We'd exhausted all commercial options for getting the cast to Denver in time for the show.

Back in Aspen, still aboard my own flight as it taxied to the gate, I relied on Jaron to keep me updated. The whole situation was looking pretty grim.

"I really don't want to cancel the show. We've never canceled anything," I sighed.

"We're not canceling," Jaron declared, resolutely. "We're going to figure out a way to get them to Denver—*trust me*. Did I ever tell you about the time that I got a military helicopter to rescue my girlfriend from Key West when she was stranded in the hurricane?"

I rolled my eyes. I had heard the story more times than I could count.

"Let me call some buddies who work in aviation. I'll keep you posted."

Sure enough, not thirty minutes later, he called back excitedly.

"I have *no* idea how I pulled this one out of my ass, but we are about to save the day right now."

He had found two planes for under ten thousand dollars in total—a fraction of the typical cost of chartering a private flight. It was expensive, but it meant the show could go on. I wired over the money without hesitation.

Joey, meanwhile, was still in jail, but Will had succeeded in convincing the judge to sentence her that day so that she wouldn't have to miss the show. The most surreal part for Joey wasn't the five hours she spent in lock-up, however. It was what happened after that. As soon as she was released, she discovered that her face had already been plastered on the home page of *TMZ*, the notorious Hollywood gossip site. It turns out that one of the airline employees was an *American Idol* fan and had contacted *TMZ* right away, in the hopes of profiting from Joey's misfortune. Other outlets picked it up, and Joey's mugshot—a shock of blue hair and just the hint of a smile—became the talk of the town. She rolled with it pretty well, all things considered.

The gang piled into the two small aircraft—a King Air 200 and a Citation Ultra—and tried to get comfortable. Yes, they were private planes but not exactly the cushy type of plane that I had enjoyed with Niia several years back. For some of the taller members of the group, it was impossible to sit upright; Rook sat in the bathroom for the entirety of the flight, as it afforded his six-foot-three frame more space than did his actual seat.

Despite a slightly delayed start, the Denver show happened

that night, and the cast thrilled the audience with an especially energetic performance—before reuniting with (and promptly passing out on) the tour bus, which had just arrived. Of everyone on that stage, however, no one gave a more inspired performance than Joey. Perhaps it was the dulling of nerves after surviving such an incredibly stressful experience earlier that day, or perhaps it was the newfound swagger that came from having her adorable mugshot splashed across the media, but whatever it was, it led to her finally securing her footing and performing with a newfound freedom and confidence. And just like that, overnight, Joey was no longer the inexperienced one.

For me, it was a proud moment, being able to watch my team pull together to make the show happen against all odds and *still* exceed expectations. Just months before, I had feared that the show was fragile enough to fall apart without my onstage presence at the piano. Now not even a case of extreme weather or a day in the slammer could stop our performers from reaching our fans. We hadn't just grown popular; we'd grown resilient.

A COMMUNITY THRIVES

ostmodern Jukebox was, by this time, a roving, rotating, ever-evolving show, but it was also a hub of artistic connectivity for a slew of performers from all around the world. These performers were brought together by their shared passion for our world of "vintage" music and desire to contribute to it, but the connections they ultimately formed with one another rarely terminated there. Our singers would hire the instrumentalists to play on their solo albums and showcases. Our instrumentalists would help one another book gigs and recording sessions between tours. And, when any of them had a concert of their own in New York City or Los Angeles, you could count on looking out over the audience and finding it stacked with other PMJ artists, there to root for their teammate, friend, and fellow creative.

Similar to the campus-like settings at top Silicon Valley tech firms, PMJ was providing an environment where talented, unique performers could meet other talented, unique performers. However, in our case, we were also sending them to see the world, meet thousands of fans, and share incredible experiences together. I often joked at rehearsals that I was "sending the kids off to school," but there was a bit of truth in the analogy. Each cast, for the most part, contained a mix of veterans and "new kids," who no doubt felt a bit of apprehension about embarking on a long tour with a group of people who already knew each other. I did my best to ensure that no one felt like the kid sitting on the curb outside a high school dance.

By late 2015, this idea of building community had become more and more central to my vision for Postmodern Jukebox. Our fall tour had more cast members coming and going throughout than ever before. Blending his Rat Pack sensibilities with insane beatboxing skills—a perfect juxtaposition of classic and modern—*American Idol* finalist Blake Lewis brought the house down as emcee in his hometown of Seattle. Sara Niemietz and Aubrey Logan made their debuts and proved to be even more amazing live than they were on video. Maiya Sykes sang her powerful take on "Creep" for the very first time on tour to tears and a massive standing ovation. PMJ veterans like Robyn, Morgan, and Haley appeared at select shows throughout, and when they did, they were treated like royalty. Our show was often described as "*Saturday Night Live* for singers," and hopefuls from around the world were sending me unsolicited audition videos. Between them and the various tap, swing, and burlesque dancers who looked to our music for inspiration, it was clear that a movement was starting to take shape around us.

To further encourage the growth of this community, I decided to run a singing competition of my own.

"I'm going to run a *PMJ Search*," I told Adam, who by now had played more shows than any other performer and was taking on more responsibilities within the group. "We'll have singers upload videos of themselves singing to our karaoke tracks, and the winner will get to do a video with us."

"Perhaps you can offer Simon Cowell–style commentary on each performance, too," Adam wryly suggested. "Delivered from a chair that spins around. With a buzzer, of course."

Adam knew of my disdain for reality television competitions and enjoyed pointing out this incongruity whenever my own ideas veered questionably close to their terrain. My own hypocrisy notwithstanding, we wound up receiving several hundred submissions in a matter of weeks. Singers from all over the world entered, putting their own spin on some of the best-loved PMJ tracks. Some of them dressed up in period-authentic costumes, others played musical instruments, and still others included pets and family members in their videos. Although a few novice vocalists entered, most were skilled performers. Some of them were flat-out incredible. Caleb Lafaitele from Australia shocked us all with his fantastic vocals on "Stacy's Mom," an entry that our cast passed around while on tour in Australia. Tara Louise performed a version of "I Want It That Way" that made Shoshana, the featured singer from our version, beam with pride. Picking a contest winner was extremely difficult, but one entry had resonated particularly with me for its simplicity: Taylor Swift's "Blank Space," as sung by Holly Campbell-Smith of Scotland.

Holly was a recently married young mother, with a charming demeanor and a love of music. Her friends had urged her to participate in the contest, and she decided to give it a shot, even though she hadn't performed in years. She recorded her entry in her kitchen, using the onboard mic and camera on her phone. It was a beautiful and unique rendition and a very memorable entry. I could certainly relate to having to resort to recording in your kitchen.

We announced Holly as our winner and flew her from Scotland to Los Angeles to record a PMJ video with her in December 2015. Since we didn't think to give her a letter to show state officials, she had trouble getting through customs and was detained in Ireland; as luck would have it, the officer in charge of her was a PMJ fan and let her go, with a request that she pass along a few of his song ideas to me. (I'm not sure what this says about border security.) She arrived at Bro Mountain late at night, exhausted from traveling but excited to meet us. Over the next couple days, we recorded a swing version of her wedding song—Ed Sheeran's "Thinking Out Loud." She did a fantastic job with a difficult arrangement, and her dry sense of humor made her a joy to work with. When our tour returned to Glasgow the next year, I invited Holly to sing "Blank Space" with us so that she could experience the thrill of performing onstage in front of thousands, backed by the phenomenal instrumentalists of PMJ. She loved every second of it, and the cast adored her right back.

#PMJsearch started off as a fun, lighthearted way to highlight talent from around the world, but it's become much more than that. It has continued to prove valuable in expanding the PMJ community globally (our 2016 winner, Devi-Ananda Dahm, came from Berlin, Germany), and it keeps us in touch with our identity as a grassroots movement that strives to always have the door open wide to those on the fringes of the industry. While many of our singers came onto the platform with existing fan bases built through television appearances, Broadway, and other tours, other singers came in with little or no experience whatsoever. Sometimes, the pure enthusiasm and genuine emotions of a first-timer lead to truly magical moments.

HOW TO SING FOR POSTMODERN JUKEBOX

I'm asked frequently how I identify the best performers and what characteristics singers should possess if they want to be featured with Postmodern Jukebox. More than anything else, I believe that skill, musicianship, and the elusive quality of uniqueness are the keys to success in any creative field, and singing is no exception. While skill and musicianship are obvious qualities shared by our performers, successful PMJ singers also radiate uniqueness, whether it's in vocal quality, image, or personality. It's what makes audiences not only want to listen to these singers but get to know them, too.

When I give advice to an aspiring singer who is clearly talented, I usually start by asking what makes him or her unique. Some people give me stock lines like "I was inspired by Amy Winehouse" or "I'm a Broadway singer, but I love jazz and pop, too." These are all well and good, but they aren't necessarily *unique*. I generally tell these performers to dig deeper to uncover something from their life experiences that truly sets them apart—and then draw inspiration from that.

You communicate what it is about you that's unique through your own personal brand. When I was growing up, there was a popular Sprite ad that featured the tag line "Image is nothing; thirst is everything." It's a nice thought and probably useful in marketing sugar water, but it doesn't really ring true. We make snap judgments all the time based on the information we have at hand, and in the world of entertainment, this applies tenfold. Part of presenting yourself as an artist is making sure your image is congruent with your art. This remains the case no matter the genre or how "serious" the music is. It's far easier to regard an artist as authentic if the person's dress, style, and offstage persona support his or her art.

Ariana Savalas exemplifies this ideal of consistency. Her love of cabaret and jazz, which led her to develop the witty "Arianaisms" that she peppers throughout her act, is entirely unforced. It helps, too, that she dresses like one of the "Real Housewives of 1970s Las Vegas." It just makes sense. When you see Ariana, you instantly grasp who she is as an artist. That should be a goal for any performer who wants to make a memorable impression on an audience: Be authentic, be consistent, and be unique.

RETURNING HOME

It was the summer before college, and I was wearing cargo shorts, a beaded necklace, and—probably the worst offense— spiky, frosted-tip hair. I wove through the chaos of Times Square in a hooded sweatshirt, dodging the sandwich board– wearing religious zealots, comedy club promoters, and mascots of popular costumed characters in my path. A few blocks later, above the swirling masses, I caught a glimpse of the iconic marquee of Radio City Music Hall, a historic venue that had launched careers, entertained millions, and withstood the test of time. It seemed to be a beacon of hope shining overhead, a reminder that New York City was still a city of possibility.

My friends and I weren't heading to Radio City that night, though; we were getting a quick meal at Sbarro and then making our way to Penn Station to catch a train back to our sleepy New Jersey town. The excitement of sneaking into a bar to see live music was wearing off, along with the effects of the cheap beers we had drunk, and the reality of an upcoming week of high school was setting in. *I'll be back there someday*, I thought, in between bites of overcooked spaghetti.

"Someday" turned out to be nearly twenty years later, but it came nonetheless. As we were beginning to put together the routing of the Postmodern Jukebox fall 2016 tour, I checked my email, and there it was, in the form of a forwarded message from Jaron: "October 7. Radio City Music Hall. Pretty awesome!" I stopped what I was doing and immediately alerted a few of the longtime PMJ stars to save the date. This was a cause for celebration, and I wanted to make it the most elaborate Postmodern Jukebox show in history. Naturally, I couldn't wait to tell my parents, since NYC was just a car ride away for them, and having them and my sister together for this occasion was an absolute must. After all, they were my first fans.

Believe it or not, time doesn't stop just because you book a show at Radio City Music Hall, and whatever other problems you have don't just fall away. The owner of Bro Mountain had decided to put the property up for sale and would no longer be renting it out, which meant I was—again—without a home. I briefly considered purchasing it, given its role in PMJ history, but ultimately decided to hunt for a house that better matched the PMJ aesthetic. My dream was to have not only a big dedicated space to function as the Postmodern Jukebox set but also the ultimate PMJ living room studio. In the interim, while I searched for a place to buy, I rented a string of Airbnbs to prep for the upcoming tours through Australia and New Zealand.

When I was twenty-seven and buried beneath a mountain of student loan debt, I had never even entertained the idea of someday being in a position to purchase a house. Now, just seven years later, I had to chuckle at the idea of finding myself contacting a real estate agent to view luxurious Los Angeles properties. Part of me felt silly; I probably wouldn't have any use for a freestanding home of my own if I didn't have a plan to turn it into a massive studio and hadn't had so many problems doing that with apartments. My living habits have largely gone unchanged from my

Astoria days, when more space translated (as it does still) directly into more space for me to leave my clothes on the floor.

To add to the chaos of house-hunting, PMJ had just sent the cast on its longest European tour to date, and my team and I were constantly involved in putting out logistical fires on an especially challenging run. A couple of singers and a drummer had to be replaced last minute due to illness or injury. The bus broke down several times, and the AC stopped functioning in Sofia, the capital city of Bulgaria, making it unbearably hot. Will and the rest of our tour crew did their best to cope, at one point even attempting to construct a series of makeshift air conditioners by filling Styrofoam containers with ice and running small cooling fans over the top of them. Desperate times call for desperate measures.

That's not to say that the 2016 European tour was anything less than incredible. We brought the cast to more new cities than ever before, including the Baltic nations and Russia. The president of Estonia came to our show wearing one of the "VOTE PMJ FOR A BETTER YESTERDAY" buttons we'd created in a publicity stunt to hijack the contentious 2016 U.S. election. In Moscow, Tambourine Guy made an appearance and got to experience firsthand what it feels like to be a viral star in a foreign country. (One fan kissed his head and said, "In our country...*you are superhero!*") In Estonia, our pianist and new music director Jesse Elder (another extremely talented and trusted friend from my *Sleep No More* days) played a traditional folk song and had the entire audience singing together in a moving display of unity. The cast members rotated pretty constantly through the four-month run, but Adam, Sarah Reich, and Sara Niemietz wound up playing all seventy-four shows—a particularly impressive feat when you realize that they lived on a bus on another continent for a third of the year. Haley— now also represented by Scott Mantell and ICM—was busy planning her own tour, but she made time for us and appeared in a few PMJ shows around the UK, including another sold-out date in London. On the day of legendary Beatles producer George Martin's passing, Haley and Casey sang "When I'm 64" in the encore set, our tribute to one of the greats.

But my focus wasn't on the tour. Rather, it was back in the States, where I had fully immersed myself in house-hunting mode. I looked at a number of very nice houses in Los Angeles, all with different configurations. Some of them had intricate gardens. Others had separate pool houses and outdoor bars. One of them had a garage converted into a large yoga studio (this was LA, after all). Occasionally, Rook would come along to inspect, testing each living room for its acoustics by clapping and yelling, which probably alienated more than a couple real estate agents. Most living rooms simply weren't built with music recording in mind. After a while, it became kind of disheartening. I got into a pattern of showing up and taking ten seconds to check out the living room before saying "nope" and going on my way. Meanwhile, my attempts at holding rehearsals at the Airbnb I was renting were already generating noise complaints and eviction letters. I couldn't help feeling that I was getting a little old for this.

Just when it seemed like I would have to start renting out actual recording studios like normal musicians did, I stumbled upon a house that looked picture perfect. It was much larger than I needed and nearly fifty years old, but its appearance just screamed PMJ to me—a mixture of old Hollywood and classic New York hotel design. I had my real estate agent schedule a viewing as soon as possible.

Stepping inside, the very first thought I had was *This is it; this is PMJ Manor*. Intricate millwork and exquisite finishes abounded, with wood paneling throughout. The entryway led to a cavernous great room—big enough to fit a full touring cast of PMJ musicians—replete with recording-friendly twenty-foot

231

ceilings. Behind that was yet another room, smaller yet still majestic, containing an old, speakeasy-style bar and a working fireplace. Instantly, I knew it: This was the spot.

Beyond the obvious visual appeal, the house also checked off another important box for me: It was distant enough from the neighbors that noise wouldn't be an issue. We could have tap dancers rehearsing at 3 a.m., if necessary. After a nail-biting month of negotiation on my offer, we struck a deal and went into contract. Just a week before our big show at Radio City Music Hall, Postmodern Jukebox was finally going to have a splendid, permanent place to call home.

I exited the bus and was immediately greeted by a crisp fall breeze and the familiar chaos of Times Square. *This place hasn't changed a bit*, I thought, while dodging traffic to retrieve my backpack from the luggage bay. It was the day of the show, but it hadn't really sunk in yet. I snuck around the side of the bus and caught a glimpse of my name on the marquee; it looked Photoshopped to me, as if this was all part of some practical joke. However, I didn't have time to dwell on the comedic possibilities of my life—there was something I needed to do.

The doors of the N train opened. I exited the platform and walked down a street in Astoria that I'd traveled many times before, headed to the three-story brick apartment building I'd called home for six years. But instead of turning my key in the lock, I was ringing Agatha's doorbell to extend a special invitation to my former landlady, who was never only just a landlady. Tonight was the night I was realizing my dream of headlining Radio City Music Hall, and I wanted Agatha there, as my guest of honor. It was sure to be a proud and emotional moment for us both—one that I'd want to remember forever, so I'd arranged for a camera crew to follow me and get it all on video.

I reached the open garage—her office—and there she was, at her desk, just as she had been three years before, at the start of my journey.

"Scott!!" she said with a sparkle in her eye as she opened the door. "Come here! So good to see you!"

"Hey, Agatha. It's great to see you, too." I smiled and gave her a big hug. She started talking very fast, occasionally slipping into Greek.

"You need a place to live?" she asked. "I have very nice apartment—it's twenty-one hundred dollars but for you, fifteen hundred!"

I laughed. "No, I'm just visiting today." She didn't hear, though, because she was excitedly dialing her phone.

"I must call Helena! We are having a party for Christmas, and we need piano! We pay you one hundred dollars. Stay right here—you'll talk to her!"

I started to explain that I was no longer located in New York City, but before I could get the words out, she thrust the phone at me, Helena on the other end of the line. I didn't outright refuse her friend's invitation to play at their party, but I thanked her and told her that I wasn't sure I could commit to it, and managed to extract myself from the conversation. I motioned for the video crew to come closer so they could pick up every word of what was to come next.

"Agatha," I said. "Remember the music thing I used to do in the basement, with the videos?"

"Yes?"

"Well, we've made it big time now. I'm playing at Radio City Music Hall tonight, and I'd love to have you come be my VIP guest and see the show."

Agatha shifted uncomfortably. Her eyes darted back and forth for a second, and she drew in a deep breath.

"I cannot.... The exterminator is coming, I must wait for him. No thank you."

So much for that emotional moment. I motioned to the video crew to wrap it up, and we packed up and said our good-byes. I'm not sure why I ever expected a different outcome than this. In a strange way, though, it was perfect. For isn't one of the beauties of family, after all, that we accept each other as we are?

During my time at *Sleep No More*, I had learned the value of paying attention to even the smallest visual details in a production. Their meticulously curated rooms were so well furnished with estate sale items from the 1930s that it often made guests question whether they had actually stepped through a portal into a different era. The sum of all these tiny details—an old typewriter with its original ink, the scent of a popular bourgeois fragrance from the 1930s, a flickering tube radio—combined into something whose effect was far greater than the individual parts would suggest. It was an entire world, with its own signature atmosphere that was better experienced than described.

Playing Radio City Music Hall meant that we needed a visual upgrade from our usual minimalist setup consisting of an Austrian drape and white music stands. The stage at Radio City was enormous, and we would easily get swallowed up unless we brought a bigger set piece. The set designer I hired sent me a number of gorgeous mockups, including one that seamlessly integrated Greek columns, contemporary lighting spheres, a 1940s-era bandstand, and New Orleans–evocative damask wallpaper. It was just the right visual to express the otherworldly, vintage-yet-quirky feel of the Postmodern Jukebox universe.

The show was, of course, our biggest Postmodern Jukebox concert yet, both in audience size and cast size. (If I keep emphasizing this, it's because *COME ON—Radio City!!*) Being in the birth state of PMJ also meant that the show was something of a *This Is Your Life* reunion, as cast and crew both old and new caught up with one another backstage. Morgan and Haley reconnected and reminisced over their first tour in Europe together. Drue and Steve hung out and talked about their upcoming projects. Natalie and the other dancers went over the moves for "Give It Away" with Aubrey. Casey and Tim worked out their own tambourine dance moves. Robyn and Von planned a duet version of "Thrift Shop" to showcase how important that song was to both of them. Jaron was there, excitedly telling me about a new idea he had, while suggesting, of course, that I hide the champagne so the promoters would bring us another bottle. It felt like a dream, one where people from different eras of your life were all together. Rook was on stage-manager duty and had inexplicably acquired a very large stick that he was using to point at people for emphasis. Everything had changed, and nothing had changed. When it was time to go on, Will gave his usual pre-show pep talk, but with a twist: "Congratulations to each and every one of you. I've had a blast with you guys. And tonight is *actually* the night"—here he paused for dramatic effect—"that I'm going to turn the speakers on so the audience can finally hear the show." In such a nerve-wracking setting, his humor was a relief.

From my vantage point in the wings, it looked and sounded like we were playing a PMJ show into a black hole; the stage was so gigantic that I couldn't see the audience beyond it. As emcee, Mykal hyped up the crowd and set the mood of excitement for the evening. Sara Niemietz charmed the audience with her brilliant vocals and infectious smile during "Hey Ya!" and Haley Reinhart received cheers from exuberant fans when she stepped onstage during the bass ostinato in "Seven Nation Army." The show seemed to race by—despite clocking in at a solid two hours—and before long, it was time for me to take the stage. I strode down the long corridor, passing well-wishers who worked for the venue and our promoters, and I ran into Robyn, who had just finished performing. We had both moved on in our personal lives and didn't speak all that often, but right now, tonight, it was suddenly important to me that we share a moment of recognition. After all, she'd been there at the very moment my crazy idea took off, transforming both of our lives in the process. She spoke first.

"Hey...remember when we used to make those funny You-Tube videos in your apartment?"

Robyn's mascara started to run, and I could feel my own eyes watering.

"I'm proud of you," I told her, and I was. Despite all her doubts and insecurities, she faced them head on and refused to give up on her dreams, no matter how difficult things got.

We hugged. What a crazy ride it had been.

I continued on, making my way past the crew to stand just behind the curtain as Mykal gave my introduction. I still couldn't see the crowd; part of me considered the possibility that the show wasn't real, that this was all some elaborate prank my friends had organized to mess with me. Then I heard my name, and with it, thunderous applause.

Stepping onto the stage at Radio City and looking out over the crowd of thousands, everything finally hit me. I looked out and saw the faces of so many people—people who were now on their feet, people who were strangers to me but that I recognized in an inexplicable way. It didn't feel like I had somehow managed to sneak into somewhere that I didn't belong. It didn't feel like a high school dance where I didn't have a single friend. It felt, at last, like home.

My mind flashed back to the early days of Postmodern Jukebox, when I was filming videos in Agatha's basement and paying musicians in falafel sandwiches. It hadn't been a glamorous operation, and there had been no promise of fame or fortune. What kept me going, back then, were the messages I'd receive from viewers all over the world who saw the possibilities of this project and who believed in the value of supporting real, live music in an industry that was becoming more airbrushed and overedited and inauthentic by the day.

In time, these messages of encouragement grew in number, as people told their friends and family about the crazy group of musical misfits turning today's radio hits into Golden Oldies in a living room somewhere.

Our group of performers grew.

It became a movement.

It became Postmodern Jukebox.

I pulled myself back into the present, onstage. This time, I was regretting my decision to not prepare a speech in advance; I think I mostly just uttered "Wow!" a whole lot, in awe. But my thought as I gazed out over Radio City Music Hall that night was about how these were the people who'd helped build Postmodern Jukebox into what it was today. *These* were the people who gave our collective of talented vocalists, musicians, and dancers a stage and told them, *We're here for you.*

The show finished in an appropriately grand fashion, given the prestige of the venue and how far we'd come. I took a seat at the piano and accompanied Morgan on "Take Me to Church" and Haley on "Creep." The show ended with "MMMBop," which had everyone in the cast onstage, dancing and partying. It was truly a celebration; Tim even found a kid dressed up as Tambourine Guy in the crowd and beckoned for this "Tiny Tambourine Guy" to come join us. Rook, who was assisting the stage manager and still carrying that large wooden stick around and poking things and people with it, sidled up beside me.

"Congratulations, man. This is really awesome. I'm proud of you, bro."

"I'm proud of you, too. You've helped build all this."

"So does that mean I can go out there with the rest of the cast?" he asked, half-jokingly.

"Of course, brother! You're part of the family."

He looked to the stage, then hesitated; he wasn't entirely convinced.

"I mean, I don't want to ruin the biggest show you've ever done."

I laughed. "Remember Rappin' Einstein? Remember selling your pants on our first tour? We didn't get here by doubting ourselves. Now, go out there and bring that damn stick."

We were a bunch of creeps, a bunch of weirdos who didn't fit into any of the boxes in the music industry, and yet here we were, right where we belonged.

But this night wasn't only about us. As we bowed one final time, I caught a last glimpse of all the smiling faces in the audience. They had found a place where they belonged, too. They were the people who championed my idea, who cheered for our performers, who spread the word about us, even when radio and TV hadn't—all because they believed that this community made their world a brighter, richer, more musical place. Out of all the lessons I learned on this journey, this was the final, most important one: *You can't go it alone.* Freedom doesn't come from doing what you want, whenever you want, and then abandoning ship as soon as the going gets tough. Freedom doesn't come from accumulating cash or material possessions and stuffing them away, lest they get stolen. Freedom comes from understanding that you need other people, just as other people need you, in this strange, twisting dance that is life.

In the pitch-black of night, I climbed into the back seat of my dad's car, and he drove my mother and me through the sleepy roads of the small town in New Jersey where I grew up, until we came to a stop at the family home they had built thirty years earlier. My ears were still ringing from the show, but I could hear the crickets chirping and the frogs croaking, a country lullaby. My mom hugged me good night, exhausted but all smiles. My dad shook my hand and then jokingly pretended to arm wrestle me, just like he did when I was a kid.

Upstairs, my room was exactly as it had been when I was in high school (except for the fact that my bed was now neatly made). I undressed, brushed my teeth, and climbed under the covers. It was comfortable and familiar, but I felt like it wasn't quite complete. Then I remembered. I sat up, flicked on the lights, and opened my closet door, which was full of boxes—each one a time capsule from a different phase of my life. In the corner was a familiar sight: "A Great Day in Harlem." The frame was a bit worse for wear from being moved in and out of storage, but the picture was as clear as ever. I delicately removed it from the closet, found the nail on my bedroom wall, and hung it back up.

EPILOGUE

Although I've chosen to end this story here, the story of Postmodern Jukebox continues to be written. In 2017, we launched several concurrent tours worldwide, toured our fifth continent (South America), and performed at such renowned venues as The Greek in Los Angeles, Red Rocks in Colorado, and Sydney Opera House in Australia. I signed a distribution deal with Concord Records to help spread our work further and released a "greatest hits so far" album, *The Essentials*. In late 2017, we filmed an hour-long PBS show called *Postmodern Jukebox: The New Classics*—our first televised special.

Many of our cast members have released and toured in support of their own solo albums, in addition to working with PMJ. Puddles reached mainstream television viewers when he landed an appearance on *America's Got Talent*. Tim "Tambourine Guy" Kubart won a Grammy for best kids' album.

Jaron is still working tirelessly on the project and is always coming up with ideas to help PMJ reach new audiences. He's also found joy in giving our performers advice on building their own careers and connecting them with people who can help them along the way. He doesn't get in nearly as many fights with other managers these days, either; perhaps he's mellowing out, or perhaps we just command a little more respect.

My longtime friends continue to thrive, both within and beyond the universe of PMJ. Ben met one of his heroes, Dave Matthews, at an airport overseas, and was invited to perform with him at several shows. (Turns out Dave is a PMJ fan.) Adam holds the record for most shows performed with us and leads the band on many of our tours, with help from Jesse Elder, who has now become music director for our multitude of tours worldwide. Steve—the friend from my infamous Walmart debut—got married and started his own studio, producing recordings and viral videos for Robyn, Drue, and other PMJ performers. And Rook still stays busy with PMJ in a wide variety of roles, including recording engineer, production supervisor, tour manager, and—according to the credits at the end of our PBS special—"spiritual advisor." In addition, he's become an in-demand studio tech, having helped engineer tracks for pop artists like Usher and producers like Steve Albini. During the 2017 World Series, our "Heroes" track that he engineered could be heard playing during the commercial breaks. He's certainly come a long way from the days of wearing a koala suit.

My parents still live in my hometown but travel quite a bit to visit my sister in Washington, DC, and to catch the occasional PMJ show. Inspired by my use of social media, my mom even started her own Facebook live stream, *Sunday's Storytime*, where she reads childhood favorites like *Watership Down* to her online viewers. My dad still plays the cornet, and I jam with him on songs from the '60s whenever I visit them in New Jersey. They both still call me Scotty.

As for me, I may no longer be a kid searching for his place in the world, but I'm learning new lessons every day. I'm far from perfect, and sometimes I mess things up, but these days I try to just accept this in myself and move on instead of stressing out. I'm thirty-six now, and thanks to experience, I know I'll likely never recapture the same intense rush I got from my first viral video, or from being on TV for the first time, or from playing our first concert, or from seeing my name in lights at Radio City Music Hall. And that's okay. Whenever I sit down at the piano, none of those things matter to me, anyway. My fingers instinctively know what to do, and suddenly, I'm transported to another universe, a place that has always existed to me, ever since I was twelve years old and fumbling through *Rhapsody in Blue*. Making music will always fill me with a sense of possibility.

Finally, I hope that as you, the reader, close this book (in either the literal or digital sense...this *is* 2018), you feel some small spark of profound inspiration yourself, and that the spark gradually builds into a roaring fire as you turn your own creative passions into creative pursuits. Mine is just one such story; every day, people around the world are making creative breakthroughs that change the way we live, listen, and learn. And although it may seem like these breakthroughs come about spontaneously, born from inspired bursts of clarity, the reality is that most of them make their way to the surface only after a series of disappointments, false starts, and spectacular failures. If you can find a way to smile through the letdowns, learn from the disasters, and—above all—stay loyal to the people you care about, you'll discover that you're unstoppable.

Life is messy, and we're all just a bunch of creeps and weirdos. And that's okay. We are *perfect*, just the way we are.

Now go forth and make art.

ACKNOWLEDGMENTS

Writing a book was the hardest creative project I've ever attempted. When I began, I thought that I could probably write this entire thing in about three months' time, based on my previous experience writing term papers back in college. I was off by about two years.

The first draft of this book was something of a disjointed mess of ideas and stories, and I want to first and foremost thank Amanda Brower for helping to shape it into a work that I am very proud to have written. Special thanks also to my editor, David Lamb, at Hachette for his additional editing work and guidance, my literary agent, Richard Abate, for taking an interest in my story and doing all the agent stuff required to get it published, and my entire Postmodern Jukebox team—Jaron, Scott Mantell, and Craig Bruck at ICM; my staff and crew; and our family of talented performers and collaborators—for giving me so many amazing stories to tell. And, of course, Mom, Dad, and my sister, Mollie—my first fans.